The Path of Wisdom

A Practical Guide to Extraordinary Living

John Hunt

Upper Gate Publishing
Colorado Springs, Colorado

The Path of Wisdom
A Practical Guide to Extraordinary Living
John Hunt

Upper Gate Publishing
6510A S. Academy Blvd. #169
Colorado Springs, CO 80906-8691

First Edition, 2011
ISBN 978-0-9825003-2-3
Published in the United States of America

All other scripture quotations are taken from the King James Version (KJV), which is in the Public Domain, and are adapted to be more readable or poetic, or to better convey the meaning of the proverb or the intention of the entry.

Publisher's Cataloging-in-Publication Data

Hunt, John D.
The path of wisdom, a practical guide to extraordinary living / John Hunt.
p. cm.
Includes bibliographical references and index.
ISBN 978-0-9825003-2-3
1. Self-actualization (Psychology). 2. Success--Psychological aspects. 3. Change.
4. Self-help techniques. 5. Spiritual life. I. Title.

BF637.S4 H861 2011
158.1--dc22
2009931444

This book is dedicated to my mentors. These amazing people have guided me over the course of my life: Maxcene Hunt, Robert Storrs, Ray Crawford, Scott Wenig, Bruce Shelly, Rich Robinson, John Cepin, Becky Towne, and Boyd Morris.

Your guidance and insight has shown me the way to *The Path of Wisdom*. Without you, I could not have taken this path and come to know its rewards and blessings. Thank you for repeatedly pointing me in the right direction.

There are three things that are too amazing for me, four that I do not understand: the way of an eagle in the sky, the way of a snake on a rock, the way of a ship in the heart of the sea, and the way of a man with a maiden.

—Agur, Son of Jakeh

Acknowledgements

A book is rarely the enterprise of a single person. Many people have contributed to making this book possible. And I would be mistaken if I didn't thank them.

My immense and heartfelt thanks to Paul Medved, Jim Romano, Lisa McCorkle, Jim White, Pat McCoy, Becky Towne, Bill Kemmeries, and Derek Blanton for offering their insight on early versions of the book. Your ideas and suggestions were enormously helpful and have improved this book many fold.

More thanks goes to Boyd Morris, and Paul, Jim, Lisa, and Bill for their ongoing support and enthusiasm surrounding the completion of the book. I could not have finished this work without your encouragement.

Several other people lightened my load when it came to the questions and editing. Paul Medved and Rachel Connell wrote most of the discussion questions at the end of each entry, and Bill Kemmeries edited some of the entries. I appreciate your help.

Kim Fiedler, SonLight Graphics, created the amazing book cover. I could not be happier with your incredible work.

In creating this book on wisdom, I occasionally drew upon the wisdom of others. I'm grateful to these insightful men and women. You may find their works helpful, too. But since this is not an academic or scholarly work, I did not cite them in the text. However, they are listed under "Works Used."

I'm grateful to all of you. I could not have completed this long journey without you. Because of you, this book will be available to many and make a difference in someone's life.

Contents

See the index to find the entries arranged by subject.

Foreword

How are you doing? You could answer the way nearly everyone does, "I'm fine." But people say that regardless of how they actually feel. So let me ask you again, "How are you really doing, deep down inside?" Is life a struggle? Do you feel miserable or at peace? Can you see the good, or is all of life ugly? Or maybe you don't see life as all bad; maybe you just want something more or different.

When people ask me how I'm doing, I often say, "Better than I deserve." I've come to understand what a gift life is, and how blessed I am that I don't get what I actually deserve. This does not mean I never have bad days or that things never go wrong. It simply means my perspective on life is my choice.

A person of wisdom responds to life graciously, a sort of going with the flow. He or she is able to maintain perspective in bad situations and is at peace with self and others. You may find this more relaxed and pleasant approach to life and self—if you choose to walk *The Path of Wisdom*.

Why choose wisdom's way? Well, so you can get your life together and truly prosper. Perhaps you know your flaws and want to change but don't know where to begin. Perhaps you have been through life's hardships—divorce, death of a loved one, financial crisis—and for the first time, you long to experience this world differently. And I believe this comes by choosing to walk *The Path of Wisdom*.

In this book, John Hunt points us down a path of meaningful and helpful principles and practices, all derived from the wisdom literature of *Proverbs.* Not only does he address the difficult issues of life, but he also provides practical solutions. He offers specific strategies from his life that you can begin using today to improve yourself and your life.

When John lived in Tucson, Arizona, I met with him about once a week for five years. At times he seemed overwhelmed with the struggles of life, career, and singleness. In the years since, John has found a more contented place. I have seen him grow into a more peaceful person with a wiser outlook. Does he have it all together? No, none of us does. Yet he does have a much better view of himself and reality. He has come to this place by following wisdom's way.

It's not John's theological training, but his reliance on wisdom from above (from God) that has helped him grasp wisdom's perspective. As a result, the guidance he offers in this book comes from a special vantage point, one that is able to make sense of this world. And making sense of our world, well, that's something we could all use.

For several decades, I have worked with people in a mentoring capacity, helping them to grow personally and experience life more fully. The wisdom found in this book is the type of guidance I have offered others. And, as a result, I have watched many of them become better people with better lives. The guidance found in these pages can have the same life-changing effect for you. Trust me—I've been mentoring others for a long time.

In following *The Path of Wisdom*, you will discover a more hopeful life and see yourself from an entirely new perspective—you will see yourself as blessed. And guess what, the next time someone asks you how you're doing, you'll be able to say, "Better than I deserve."

Rich Robinson, Associate Director
U.S. Military Mission, The Navigators

Introduction

Perhaps at some point you have wondered: *How did my life get to be so difficult, so chaotic, or even miserable?* I have asked myself this question many times. Frankly, I got tired of the same unwanted and unwelcome outcomes. I decided there had to be a better way. I assume you also want a more fulfilling and rewarding life. But unless we alter our patterns, behaviors, and decisions, we will remain in a hectic or despondent way of life.

The reason chaos or misery riddled much of my past is not because of hardship or failure. Everyone has those. My problem was my reactions to my problems. Typically, I responded to difficult situations in unhealthy ways or with destructive choices.

And what about you? Are you or a friend in a less-than-desirable position? How did it happen? More important, how are you going to get out of it or keep from returning to it? If you're anything like me, you can probably relate to one or both of the following situations:

1. When it comes to the problems and issues in your life, whether dealing with criticism, meager finances, or some other adversity, *you tend to make poor choices*, and do so repeatedly—only compounding the problem.
2. When it comes to the difficulties and inconsistencies of life, whether dealing with disagreements, marriage problems, or some other relationship, *you react based upon destructive patterns from your past*, and do so repeatedly—only making matters worse.

Fortunately, for you and me, there is a better way to handle life's difficulties—*wisdom*. Typically, people think of wisdom as esoteric, but, no, wisdom is practical. It guides a person into making right choices and offers sensible steps to living well.

Those who follow wisdom's way live with confounding ease. They seem content in all circumstances and comfortable with all people. They possess something that the rest of us want and need—peace of mind. The need, desperate at times, for individuals and families to bring some degree of calm to their troubled or frenzied existence sends people searching for help. *The Path of Wisdom* is that help. If you found books like *Don't Sweat the Small Stuff* or *The Purpose Driven Life* helpful, then you'll benefit from this book too.

Is work hectic? Is your family frazzled? Is your life miserable? Find welcome relief in reordering work, family, and life around a simpler, more enriching way—*The Path of Wisdom*. Most people desire success at work or in business, but in these pages, you will gain something far better—fruitful living. The modern family can't seem to resist compounding life with much and more and will welcome wisdom's more fulfilling approach. The single person aches with loneliness and the desire to be married, but along this path they will find contentment. For those who are frantic, overwhelmed, or miserable, *The Path of Wisdom* provides peace, satisfaction, and fulfillment.

Come and walk with me on this path to a better life. Our starting point, the trailhead for the path of wisdom, begins in ancient Mesopotamia. The sages of this region wrote what is known as wisdom literature. We will look at what these ancients said to see what will help us to live well today.

The Egyptians, Sumerians, Babylonians, and Hebrews each had their own wise men and women, but we will focus our attention on the writings of the Hebrews, in particular a book called *Míshlê Shlomoh*, which means *The Proverbs of Solomon*.

From *Proverbs* we find these words on wisdom and life: "Wisdom says, 'Come, eat my food and drink my wine. Leave your simple ways, and you will know what it means to truly live.' "

The themes of life and death in *Proverbs* refer to the human quest for satisfaction. For eons, people have tried to find it by extending their days or multiplying their wealth, but the word *life* in *Proverbs* encompasses the fullness of life, its intensity and quality. Wisdom's tree of life sustains, delights, and blesses; those who eat from it find life worth living no matter the circumstances they face.

The Path of Wisdom includes 100 brief entries based upon practical insights found in the pages of *Proverbs.* With gentle, supportive, powerful suggestions about relationships, finances, success, purpose, pleasure, work, stress, and much more, these entries offer practices and principles that provide true wealth and real peace. These entries also serve as an introduction to God's ways for living well. You might say that God is behind the scenes, or more precisely, that he is behind the sayings.

The strategies and principles in these pages are the ones I have found most helpful in my own attempt to live better, though I come up short more often than I care to admit. Fortunately, for both you and me, the practices here point us down a path. We do not have to arrive at the destination today or even tomorrow; we can simply take comfort in knowing we are moving in the right direction.

Use this book for personal reflection or for group study. Feel free to start at the beginning of the book or skim the contents or subject index in the back for topics that interest you. The questions at the end of each entry, the subject index, and the resource guide are provided to empower you (or your group) to practice and possess peace and satisfaction rarely experienced in this frenetic and distraught culture.

I'm honored that you have chosen to walk this way with me. I hope to be a worthy guide. If you will not only read, but also put into practice (walk the path) wisdom's ways, you will likely find the more pleasing and gratifying life you desire.

Your fellow pilgrim down a better path,
John Hunt

1.

Wisdom Offers a Better Way to Live

Wisdom says, "Come, eat of my bread and drink of my wine. Forsake your simple ways, and [you will know what it means to truly] live" (Proverbs 9:5–6).

Most people have little problem going to a "sage," some type of advisor or counselor for guidance or help. The people of ancient Mesopotamia were no different. They often turned to their wisdom writings for sage direction. The writings of one people in this region, the Hebrews, will be our focus. While their work of wisdom comprises a number of volumes, our attention will be on a book called *Proverbs*.

Proverbs asks of every thought or action: Is this wise? The words *wise* or *wisdom* may conjure pictures of gray-haired old men muttering obscure philosophical maxims, but that is almost the opposite of what *Proverbs* means. Wisdom is practical and down-to-earth. Wisdom teaches you how to live.

Wisdom is not reserved for the brainy elite. Wisdom offers her fruit to the naïve and ignorant, giving to them common sense and prudence. She offers to the young and impetuous, discretion and sound advice. And to the wise or knowledgeable, she gives counsel and even greater wisdom. She welcomes anyone to her table. Anyone can become wise.

Typically, you gain wisdom through one of two means: years of "trial and error" or the proven experience of others. If you live by "trial," then through much of your life, you will be forced to live with the consequences of the "errors." But if you heed the advice of others, there are clear advantages. Unburdened with the consequences of earlier mistakes, you can live freer and fuller here and now. Heeding the voices of those who have gone before you makes sense, much sense.

The wise men who wrote *Proverbs* learned life the hard way. They will be our guides down *The Path of Wisdom*. If we can learn from their errors, so as not to repeat them, we can save ourselves from many miseries.

The person who lives according to wisdom's way will know wisdom's blessing. Satisfaction, prosperity, peace of mind—these are the fruits that wisdom sets at her table, if only we will stop and eat. *Proverbs* frankly concedes, however, that few will choose the wise path. It is easier to live carelessly and rashly. The question for you and me is this: Will we choose wisdom's way?

Walking the path of wisdom . . .

1. What does the word *wisdom* mean? Why is this an important quality to possess?
2. Why is it important to heed, absorb, and internalize the principles of wisdom? How can you accomplish this?
3. How can you become wise? What difference can wisdom make in your life?

2.

Accept Wisdom's Invitation to Adventure

There are three things that are too wonderful for me, surely, four that I do not understand: the way of an eagle in the air, the way of a snake on a rock, the way of a ship in the heart of the sea, and the way of a man with a maiden (Proverbs 30:18–19).

What do you find to be amazing, wonderful, or unexplainable? The great sage Agur made some observations on four things from nature, including human nature, that were too vast for him to understand.

Even in our scientific age, which has taken much of the mystery out of many marvels, we still watch mesmerized as an eagle soars over a lake or a garter snake glides across the ground. How a ship in the heart of the sea, let's say in a storm, somehow manages to stay afloat is a wonder. That a man ever obtains a woman's affection or hand in marriage (or vice versa) is the greatest mystery of them all.

But more is going on here than just the observation of natural wonders. Agur has given us something of a riddle. What do these four things have in common?

My favorite explanation is this: None of the four are going over old territory. The eagle, the snake and the ship go where there is no path, and anytime a man moves toward a woman, most men would say, he is moving into uncharted territory.

The way traveled by each of these creatures has no path. These four wondrous creatures illustrate trailblazing as a way of life. Similarly, the path of wisdom is a way of uncommon ground, setting a course where there is no track. Wisdom calls us to view and approach life as an adventure, like a ship at sea or a man pursuing a woman. Wisdom leads us in directions we would not normally take. The typical life follows the masses, but wisdom blazes her own trail.

Wisdom's path offers adventure, challenge, and reward. She invites us to take the uncommon way. Accept the call to adventure. Live your life differently. The options are endless: take risks, meet people, form bonds, stretch yourself, change up your routine, allow yourself to be vulnerable. These suggestions, and many others, are covered in this book. And if you follow them, you are bound to blaze the trail of wisdom.

Walking the path of wisdom . . .

1. If the path of wisdom is a wondrous way that leads to adventure and blessing, why don't we take that way more often?
2. Are there opportunities for adventure in your life that you have been unwilling to take? Why?
3. What will you do differently this week to take the path of wisdom, to live your life differently?

3.

The Pursuit of a Good Name Is a Good End

A good name is more desirable than great riches; to be esteemed is better than silver or gold (Proverbs 22:1, NIV).

When I was a boy, my dad consistently reminded me to keep the Hunt family name. By that he meant deal honestly with people and keep my word. He wanted our family to have a good reputation. When you have a good name, you can expect others to esteem you and hold you in high regard, not because of status or celebrity but because of your character.

While the pursuit of silver or gold is not necessarily wrong, and some have even argued that it's good, it is not what is best. What is more desirable than money or wealth? A good name. We can pursue this good name, this higher end, through the practice of wisdom, which is a matter of doing and being—doing the right things and being the right kind of person.*

The person who does the right things is the one who heeds wisdom's standard of right and wrong. Wisdom's voices instruct from without (natural law) and from within (conscience), but to hear wisdom's guidance, you will need to shut out the clamoring world and take time for spiritual thought. One of the most important things you can do for yourself (and others) is to set aside time for personal and spiritual reflection.†

The right kind of person is the one who masters himself. Any person who conquers anything within that keeps him from attaining what he holds dearest has mastered himself. He realizes that the great men and women of history have been those who struggled against their inner weaknesses and subdued them with their will.

Once a person has learned to effectively govern himself, he can begin practicing relational mastery. This means relating to others without unhealthy dependency or destructive control but with mutually beneficial and empowering interaction. This new approach to relationships opens new possibilities for intimacy, productivity, and prosperity.

Until a person realizes it is his privilege to live the life committed to him in the highest possible manner, he is merely passing through the years. By the pursuit of a good name, he can make his years meaningful and add to them something more valuable and lasting than the material.

Walking the path of wisdom . . .

1. What value do you place on having a good name?
2. What values, principles, or practices do you struggle to make a part of your person for the sake of your good name?
3. What can you do to master these struggles and make your good name more secure?

NOTES:

* Becoming a person of character, someone with a good name, can be elusive. One reason is that our unhealthy beliefs and thoughts govern our actions. *Affirming the Path* will assist you in creating the right inner "framing" necessary for living out the principles and practices of *The Path of Wisdom.* Visit the resource page: www.ThePathofWisdom.com/resources.htm.

† One of the best approaches for reflection and hearing wisdom is the discipline of centering prayer. Find the free article on this enriching spiritual discipline among other resources: www.ThePathofWisdom.com/resources.htm.

4.

Accept That You Don't Know Everything

Hold fast to instruction; do not let her go. Guard her, for she is your life (Proverbs 4:13).

Before anyone can learn the path of wisdom, he has to admit he doesn't know everything. The Hebrew wisdom teachers tell of three types of people who have a hard time accepting this fundamental truth.

First is the simple. The simple person is not dumb; she simply lives her life without thinking or listening. The "simpleton" is content with blissful ignorance, living life without thought or regard for her actions, attitudes, or speech. The simple person is rarely persuaded to change because she doesn't listen. Instruction is lost on the simpleton—"It goes in one ear and out the other."

The second is the fool. Again, this is not a dimwitted person, but someone who rejects the insight of others. He has made a conscious decision to live by his own light, independent of others' advice or authority. While the simple person may not listen, the fool hears it all right but rejects it—"He is wise in his own eyes."

Then there is the mocker. The mocker combines "rightness" with arrogance, a sense of superiority. Like the fool, he knows it all, but he also thinks he knows better. He regards anyone who differs with contempt. He lives by his own rules and all other rules "are made to be broken." The simple fail to listen, the fool rejects instruction, but the mocker derides those who differ—"It's my way or the highway."

At different times, I've played all three roles, but not one of them has gotten me anywhere. If you find in yourself any of the practices or qualities of the simple, the fool, or the mocker, decide today that the next time correction or instruction comes your way, you will seriously consider it. Typically, we are blind to our own faults, but what we cannot see, others most assuredly can. Let others be your eyes.

I know all too well that humbling one's self is not easy. Going from knowing it all to admitting that I could still learn a few things takes a change in attitude. According to Solomon, the inability or flat refusal to accept correction, guidance, and knowledge from others only harms us (Proverbs 15:32), but the one who accepts correction finds life. Welcome instruction—and improve *your life.*

Walking the path of wisdom . . .

1. Do you see any of the tendencies of the simple, the fool, or the mocker in you? How can you overcome them?
2. Why is instruction highly regarded by those who are wise? How does instruction help a person?
3. Think over the last two years of your life? To whom do you listen? Who has the greatest influence on you?

5.

Seek Humility as a Position of Strength

A person's prideful heart will bring him low, but honor will uphold a person with humility (Proverbs 29:23).

Our culture derides humility; it is viewed as weakness. But according to wisdom, humility is actually a position of strength. It is hard to imagine how being humble can accomplish anything but humiliation, but wisdom provides a new understanding of this unassuming attitude.

Pride is the obvious opposite to humility. Most people see pride for what it is: a futile attempt to compensate for insecurities and self-doubt. The irony is that pride accomplishes the opposite of what the proud person intends. Pride demands honor while bringing dishonor. This makes pride the true position of weakness. Conversely, this makes humility the true position of strength.

Humility strengthens a person's standing. Humility is strength under self-restraint. When there is a dispute, you don't have to be right. When there is a quarrel, you don't delve into pettiness. Humility allows you to take the high road, to be the bigger person. Such actions will gain you the respect of others and strengthen your position the next time there is a disagreement.

Humility strengthens a person's appeal and character. The humble person is able to admit faults and wrongs, which is particularly attractive. Furthermore, humble people are more likely than the proud to grow from their mistakes or to learn from correction.

Humility strengthens a person's body. *Proverbs* says that someone who is not proud will be healed in his body. The word *body* in Hebrew thought actually refers to the whole person, which means that humility and wholeness go together. If you want peace of mind, contentment, and wholeness, then practice humility.

Humility strengthens a person's relationships. Most people relate easily to a humble person. Also, the humble person has no problem exalting others. Thus, people want to be around a person of humility.

My tendency is not humility but pride, and I must consciously guard against it. If you're like me, then let's diligently pursue humility. When we feel compelled to boast or speak arrogantly, let's consciously stop ourselves. Instead, we can say something that would exalt another. The next time we start to think more highly of ourselves than we ought, we can think instead of the contributions of others. Whenever we feel compelled to assert our rights, we can instead grant another's rights. With diligence, we can increase humility and strengthen our position.

Walking the path of wisdom . . .

1. How does the broader culture tend to view humility?
2. How might humility accomplish more for an individual than pride?
3. Which of the ways describing humility as a strength do you find easy to believe? Which one do you find hard to believe? Why?

6.

Make Honor Your Highest Value

He who pursues what is right and gracious finds life, prosperity and honor (Proverbs 21:21).

Princes of the past and celebrities of today have been granted special recognition, but this is not what *Proverbs* means by *honor*. Most people are familiar with the importance of honor in Asian cultures. This honor has little to do with one's high status or position and everything to do with how one lives. This view closely parallels the ancient Hebrew understanding. Honor had to do with acting honorably.

A person of honor is one whose character makes him worthy of the esteem of others. The person who makes honor his highest value is going to act and live rightly. The Hebrew sages had some things to say about being a person of honor.

An honorable person gains understanding and grace (Proverbs 3:3–4). She seeks out the wisdom and knowledge of others and always remembers that knowledge can "puff up." Similarly, an honorable person responds with grace in difficult circumstances and gratitude when things are going well.

An honorable person calls what is right, right. He delights in what is right, and does what is right no matter how small it might seem, no matter what others might think, or no matter who is watching (Proverbs 28:12). Similarly, an honorable person means and does what he says.

An honorable person does not seek flattery or exalt himself. If any praise comes his way, it is not from his own lips, but by the lips of others. And when praise does come, he is not proud and gives the credit to others (Proverbs 29:23).

An honorable person is known by the way she treats others. She cares for basic needs, speaks up for those without a voice, and keeps confidences. She also seeks peaceful solutions and extends grace—especially when she is wronged (Proverbs 27:10).

What people value varies greatly, but let's make honor one of our highest values. Honor has to do with living rightly. For example, we could act on our good intentions, embrace a new attitude, or try out a new role. Proper attitudes and actions will make us more honorable and our influence will grow. We may never hold a position that demands recognition, but real honor is within our grasp.

See also entry 85.

Walking the path of wisdom . . .

1. Who or what does the culture tend to honor? What do you think of cultural attempts to ascribe honor?
2. Which of the depictions of an honoring person do you find the easiest to practice? Which do you find more difficult to practice?
3. What can you do to become a person worthy of the honor of others?

7.

Self-Control Increases Your Personal Power

Any person who lacks self-control is like a city whose walls are broken down (Proverbs 25:28).

Much of the "get ahead" material on bookshelves recommends exerting one's influence on people and circumstances. Real power, however, begins not with how much we affect the external, but with how much we exert on ourselves internally. To fail here is to lack real power.

At any point in a person's life, he either possesses inner strength, like the strong wall of a city, or he shows himself weak in character.* If he surrenders to his weaknesses, he is *like a city whose walls are torn down*—powerless and overrun. He leaves himself open to any attack coming from life's difficulties or temptation's lures. Conversely, day by day, as a person masters the opposing elements within him and gains dominion over his natural inclinations, he builds inner strength that cannot be easily swayed. He comes to have an internal wall as a checkpoint against harmful influences.

Too often whims, passions, and desires control people—especially in a culture of immediate gratification. Many people live ruined or dissatisfied lives because they rushed into something that seemed at the moment good, desirable, or pleasurable. Living by the passion of the moment may satisfy for the moment, but how often does it leave one feeling empty, ruined, or something worse? We teach children that they can't have everything they want. Why do we think the rule changes when we become adults?

A person can attain self-control by carefully studying herself to find the weak points in her internal wall. Is it melancholy, fear, pride, selfishness, anger, laziness, worry, or some other human failing? Then each day, moment by moment, she can work to master even the slightest occurrence of the unwanted flaw.

A person can also develop self-control when he becomes mindful instead of emotional. In the moment, in the heat of passion, at the point of gratification, he chooses mindfulness. Mindfulness does not charge ahead without thought or reflection; it stops to think. A small but continued price made each day to weigh the consequences or options fosters a habit of making mindful decisions.

We show ourselves to be people of inner strength when we exercise self-control. The more we demonstrate that our inner world is in order, the more we improve our position with the rest of the world. Others will come to see us as a city with a strong tower—as a person of strength.

Walking the path of wisdom . . .

1. Why is self-control so important? What are the benefits of self-control?
2. What internal weaknesses tempt you the most? Why?
3. In what situations have you lost control? In what situations would it be beneficial or even essential to exercise self-control?

NOTES:

* Calmness is the crown of self-control, a peace and restfulness at the depths of our nature. The calm person lives in serenity and strength, unruffled regardless of the situation or temptation. Crown yourself with calmness and self–control. You will discover the free chapter, *The Majesty of Calmness*, at the resource page: www.ThePathofWisdom.com/resources.htm.

8.

Be a Peacemaker Whenever Possible

Deceit is in the heart of those that devise evil, but a counselor of peace possesses joy (Proverbs 12:20).

This proverb puts peacemaking opposite evil intentions. Deceit and evil intentions cause dissension, but the peacemaker creates harmony and joy. We can choose to cause dissension or peace. When we decide to be *counselors of peace*, we get to rejoice in the resulting goodwill.

Making *peace* refers to the establishment of positive relationships with people and is a costly, sometimes painful, enterprise. When we are in conflict with another, we face the pain of apologizing or confronting. If we are not personally involved in the dispute, we may be in a position to attempt reconciliation between estranged people or groups. In this case, we face the possible pain of misunderstanding, failure, or ingratitude.

Free from deceit, counselors of peace speak honestly with people. They share and relate genuinely, even when tough issues and conflicts arise. They know that disputes are opportunities to pour the balm of peace upon irritable feelings and wounded relationships. But as much as they (and we) may want or strive for peace, it is not always possible—a harsh reality the peacemaker may have a hard time accepting.

Whether you're addressing a dispute between you and someone else or between two other parties, it's important to reduce the differences. You can do this through blending, an attempt to foster common ground or mutual understanding. Obviously, you can blend by finding the points or approaches that you (or they) agree upon. But you can also blend by using similar speech patterns or word choices. More subtly, you can blend by matching positive facial expressions, mannerisms, or posture.

After blending, you might try redirecting. That is, take the increased rapport from blending and use it to change the direction of the interaction. The rapport fostered from blending will make it easier, but not necessarily easy, to approach the areas of disagreement.

In the Hebrew commentary *Sifra* it says, "He who practices peace is a child of the world to come." Presumably, the world to come is a world of peace, and we make that future a present reality when we foster greater harmony between people. As counselors in reconciliation, we make life and relationships less divisive and more joyful, but we also accept that sometimes peace in this world is not possible—no matter how hard we try.

See also entry 51.

Walking the path of wisdom . . .

1. Is there someone with whom you need to make peace or assist in peacemaking?
2. How would blending or redirecting techniques be helpful in bringing peace? What other relational skills might you employ to assist in peacemaking?
3. What kind of results can you expect in either seeking peace or in being a peacemaker?

9.

Wealth is Wanting What You Have

He who is full loathes honey, but to the hungry even what is bitter tastes sweet (Proverbs 27:7, NIV).

This proverb is not a truism about food, but a parable on possessions. Those who go hungry (the poor) are in contrast to those who are full (the rich). The full person, it would appear, is never satisfied; he hates the *sweet* things set before him. Once the full get what they want, there is still something else they desire. The insatiable need to acquire has a way of making the full feel unhappy.

Only a false piety, however, throws wealth and prosperity onto the dust heap of vanities. After all, most of us want affluence. But when we allow ourselves to become dissatisfied, especially when we have many possessions, we actually increase our poverty. "We permit what we lack to poison the waters of what we have" (William George Jordan, *The Power of Purpose,* 59).

An impoverished person is not one who has little, but the one who never thinks she has enough. A wealthy person is not the one who has much, but the one who sees just how much she really has—*even what is bitter tastes sweet.*

If I wish to be truly wealthy, I need to accept what I have. For instance, instead of wishing I had a new car, I could be grateful for the vehicle in my driveway. I could complain that I'm not making enough money, or I could think on how fortunate I am to make a living. Rather than wishing I could take that dream trip to the Bahamas, I could find ways to enjoy myself closer to home.

The funny thing is, when you want what you have you end up getting more anyway. If you're grateful you have a car, you'll see the car you have as sufficient for your needs. If you're glad to have a job, you are more likely to perform well and increase your income. If you can enjoy yourself close to home, you'll be in the habit of enjoying yourself whether near or far.

Some people seem to bear the burden of wealth and success without it adversely affecting them. They remain unspoiled by their money or possessions for one simple reason: No matter what or how much they have, it is enough. Do we wish to be well-off? Then instead of wanting more, let us appreciate what we already have. When we want what we have, then we are truly wealthy.

Walking the path of wisdom . . .

1. What factors might contribute to becoming wise and obtaining true wealth?
2. What are some things you've complained about that you could be grateful for instead?
3. Do you feel content with what you have? How can you foster a greater appreciation for what you have?

10.

Kindness Douses the Angry Flame

A soft answer turns away wrath, but harsh words stir up anger (Proverbs 15:1).

Not too long ago, a friend and I differed on some issues that included our mutual involvement and responsibility. Our conversation was combative. I would dispute and blame him; he in turn did the same to me. Each of us had valid points, but a breakthrough did not occur until one of us decided to speak kindly from the heart, and it was my friend, not me, who took this tact. His approach changed the course of the conversation. He softened, so I softened. We became less accusatory, and each took more personal responsibility. We were able to move on to a constructive resolution to our differences.

Solomon says a gentle tongue breaks another's bones (Proverbs 25:15). This might sound paradoxical, but it illustrates the power of gentleness over harshness. Many a resistant heart have been softened by kindness or patience. A gentle answer is the water that quenches, while harsh words add fuel to the fire, just as assuredly as twisting someone's nose produces blood (Proverbs 30:33).

One Hebrew story illustrates the power of gentle words. The prophet Elijah fled from the corrupt Queen Jezebel, who sought to kill him after he successfully humiliated the prophets of Baal. God directed Elijah to go to a cave and await his instruction. At the cave, a powerful wind ripped away the rocks, but the voice of God was not in the wind. After the wind, a rumbling earthquake shook the cliffs, but the voice of God was not in the tremors. After the quake, a consuming fire flashed past the cave, but the voice of God was not in the fire. After the fire, came a gentle whisper, and there in the whisper was the voice of God. He then corrected Elijah for fleeing. But instead of harsh words, God used a gentle whisper.

Unfortunately, our natural inclination is to return strife for strife. We succumb to irritation, insist on the last word, respond harshly, claim our rightness, and declare good reason to be angry. Each side stakes his position; neither side surrenders the slightest will. Passion and pride on both sides strike each other, and the result is an untamed flame that injures them both.

Gentle and healing words gain a double victory, first over self and then over our brother or sister. Let's possess a demeanor that is gentle and not easily irritated. If someone begins in anger, let us refrain from continuing the strife. The Roman philosopher Seneca put it this way: "Let dissension begin with others, but reconciliation from you."

Walking the path of wisdom . . .

1. Can you think of a situation when you used harsh words, and it only made matters worse?
2. Can you think of a situation when you used gentle words, and the whole tenor of the conversation or even the relationship changed?
3. Why do you think we have such a difficult time using and preferring gentle words instead of harsh words?

11.

Find Satisfaction in Your Labors

Someone who is lazy craves and gets nothing, but the desires of the laborer are fully satisfied (Proverbs 13:4).

Men and women are not born as stones, lacking animation, nor are they machines moved only by passive energy. An active, even creative, force operates within humanity. We are fulfilled and satisfied when we are in motion, which includes play and work. When it comes to work, some consider it a curse, but work has value and adds meaning to our lives.

Some socialites, elitists, and certain people among the wealthy, seem to look with reproach upon people who have to work. With a less-than-subtle confidence, these snooty people take delight in their external adornment, not realizing that the condition of their hearts makes them far uglier than those they despise. Contrary to the belief of these self-deluded souls, there is nothing wrong with labor. In fact, a life of ease kills a person's appetite and keeps him from seeking, striving, and attaining the very things that bring a sense of accomplishment and fulfillment. A life alienated from work craves something but gets nothing.

In the world of *Proverbs*, the reward for work was obvious. If people did not work, they did not eat. Hunting and gathering, planting and reaping had an immediate value for the ancient Hebrew. He could see the end product of his labors. This is not the case for the modern worker. In an industrial and informational society, rarely is the pay immediate or the reward concrete.

Frequently, a job becomes a way to get maximum pay for minimal effort, but work doesn't have to be so meaningless. The solution for you, the worker, is to find purpose in your job, even if the purpose is just to improve a weakness in your character. Ask yourself, "Why am here, at this job?" And hopefully you come up with an answer other than, "To get a pay check."

Work is that human activity that corresponds to God's providential care in this world. And until a person opts to work as part of this creative and sustaining force, the idea that there is satisfaction in labor will sound hollow. Once the idea is put to the test, however, it becomes like a seed and blossoms into a thousand flowers of blessing. Lasting satisfaction comes to those who are diligent in their labors.

Walking the path of wisdom . . .

1. How do certain segments of the culture view work? What does the culture in general think about work?
2. What do you think of wisdom's view of work? How does the type of work done today make it difficult to find meaning in work?
3. How do you motivate yourself to work? What are the advantages to doing work when there's work to be done?

12.

If the Spirit Is Broken, Make the Heart Glad

A glad heart makes a radiant countenance; but when the heart is full of sorrow, the spirit is low (Proverbs 15:13).

According to the sage, sadness in the heart brings the spirit low. We have all felt low in spirit before. Sometimes low feelings are due to tragic or difficult circumstances, as in the loss of a loved one. Many times, however, sad feelings are self-inflicted by negative thoughts.* If we wish to lift the spirit, then we should make the heart glad, and we make the heart glad by changing our thoughts.

Any time you feel badly take notice of your thoughts. If they are obsessive or negative, boil them down to one main thought. Write it down and make a list of positive thoughts and actions to answer and counter your pessimistic cognition. In coming up with your list, you may find it helpful to imagine someone you care deeply about voicing your same terrible thoughts. What would you say to him? What steps would you tell her to take?

For example, let's say that a single guy named Rob is feeling lonely. His damaging thinking is telling him that being alone is not a good status in life. He makes a list to counter his thought: *Being without a wife or girlfriend is terrible.*

1. Being alone allows me to do things I could not do if I were married. Don't live life waiting for a supposedly better situation. Just live. Action: Sign up for the "Good Samaritan" trip to Rwanda.
2. It would be nice to have a relationship but not necessary. Having a woman in my life is a want not a need.
3. Being alone is better than being in a bad relationship or marriage. Some of my friends are miserable in their marriages.

4. While I'm looking for the right person, I can work on becoming the right person. Then when I meet her, I will wow her. Action: Register for dating conference.
5. I can date whomever whenever. Action: Call Angie and ask her out to dinner.
6. I can enjoy my own company, and that's exactly what I'm going to do. Action: Go to lunch and a movie by myself.

Take a look at what Rob will do as an answer to his negative thought on being alone: View singleness as a blessing; take a trip to Rwanda; go to a conference on dating; become a better person; call a woman; go on a date; live life more fully; enjoy a good movie. An amazing turnaround, I would say. Now it's your turn to counter your negative thoughts and make the heart glad.

Walking the path of wisdom . . .

1. What situations tend to trigger negative thoughts for you? What negative elements should you consistently avoid?
2. What positive thoughts or activities regularly feed your mind and make you glad?
3. How might you discipline yourself to think more positively?

NOTES:

* If negative emotions control your life and weigh you down, you can beat them and feel good again. My free tool on overcoming depression and other negative emotions will show you how. It's available among other resources at: www.ThePathofWisdom.com/resources.htm.

13.

Giving to Others Is Refreshing

A generous man will prosper; he who refreshes others will himself be refreshed (Proverbs 11:25, NIV).

The holy book of the ancient Hebrews, the Torah, instructed them to set aside every seventh year, called a Sabbath year, as a year of rest for the land and its people. Every seventh Sabbath year (or the 50th year) was declared a Year of Jubilee. During Jubilee each community was to take a break from doing things as usual and set straight the wrongs. Generally, this meant releasing servants, returning confiscated lands, and forgiving debts.

The Jubilee reminded the Hebrews that everything enriching their lives—money, family, friends, property, possessions—were gifts on loan from above. They were given many blessings to enjoy but none to fully possess. This incredible concept remained just a concept. Why? Well, the Hebrews rarely practiced Jubilee. This failure was to their loss because returning land or releasing servants was meant to be as much a celebration for the giver as the receiver.

If we cling to what we have, as if it's solely our own, we will undoubtedly be less than thrilled to give it away. But if we can see our belongings as ours to manage rather than possess, it will not be as difficult to let them go. My dad reminded me one day of the value of giving. He owned a coin-operated Laundromat, and on one of the washers he had painted the words: "All proceeds for this washer go to the *Make a Wish Foundation*." My dad was willing to let go of his proceeds.

One theologian asks about giving: "Whose good is it to be, mine or my neighbor's?" The answer implied is that my giving should be for my neighbor's good. But our wisdom teacher is pragmatic (without thinking the end justifies the means) and suggests that giving can be equally good for the giver. What a great motivator for being generous! Giving is an act that *refreshes* and blesses both the giver and receiver.

Though the proverb does not specify how the benefactor will be refreshed, we can assume the reward will come through the natural order of things, such as the inward satisfaction of helping or the outward satisfaction of earning respect. Perhaps the prosperity will come through the enjoyment of our portion, even if the portion is smaller, which explains how it is possible to be prosperous when having less.

Those who practice generosity will have all the things that others seek in possessing; they will have prosperity and refreshment. The truly prosperous person is the generous person.

See also entry 71.

Walking the path of wisdom . . .

1. How do you feel when someone is generous toward you? Why?
2. How is it possible that the generous person acquires the very things (prosperity, blessing, etc.) the tightfisted person wants?
3. What are the benefits or rewards that come with being generous? How can you develop generosity? How can you use what you have to give to others?

14.

You Can't Expect to Change Others

Though you grind a fool in a mortar... his foolishness will not be forced out of him (Proverbs 27:22).

Most people have heard good advice and thought: *I wish so-and-so was around to hear this.* Perhaps this person isn't a fool, as described in the proverb, but apparently there's still something about so-and-so you would change. I have heard single women talk about a man of interest, that he comes up short somehow, and then one of them says, "But I can fix him." These single women are no different than any of us. We all have someone we would like to change.

We look at what certain people do, and we can't understand how they can be so foolish. We would like them to change, perhaps expect them to change, and that's not necessarily wrong, but when we *need* them to change or try to *fix* them, then we inadvertently create problems. You see, needing someone to change is not a need we can affect, and trying to change someone is beyond our control.

Any attempt to change someone is likely to cause issues. You think you're doing this "foolish" person a favor, but she won't see it that way. No matter how hard you strive to grind the "folly" out of her, the folly will remain. Why? Most people resist any coercion to be something or someone else. More than likely, she will not want to be what you think is better. She may even come out fighting, and say things like, "Just who do you think you are?"

If trying to change someone is sure to fail, why do we make the attempt? Well, we have needs or desires we want met, and we usually want them from a certain person or relationship. But this is not a healthy or wise way to meet our needs.

This is not to say we shouldn't correct people if they need to be corrected. *Proverbs* is replete with the benefits of a timely rebuke, but that's different than trying to change someone so he or she better suits you. You can edify, encourage, and even challenge others, but if you try to grind the foolishness out of them, you're sure to be disappointed or worse.

You can't change others, but you can change yourself. Your effort to adjust yourself might influence others and make it more likely that they will change. But again, you can't make this a need or objective; it is simply beyond your control. Put aside the need or attempt to fix people, and you'll save yourself and your relationships from much hassle.

Walking the path of wisdom . . .

1. Do you know someone you would like to change? What would you change? Do you *need* this person to change?
2. Have you ever created more problems in a relationship by trying to change someone? Or maybe someone tried to change you? How did that make you feel?
3. How does correcting someone differ from trying to change him or her? How might changing yourself have an influence on others and whether they change?

15.

Set Aside Your Right to Be Right

A fool finds no pleasure in understanding, but delights in airing his own opinions (Proverbs 18:2, NIV).

Occasionally, I hear a child, corrected for something she said, come back with, "I can say whatever I want; it's a free country." Even from an early age, we defend our right to express our point of view. We defend our right to voice our opinion. But this defensive attitude is not necessary.

It's true, we can say whatever we want, but asserting that right isn't always the best option. Just consider the last time someone pointed out that he was right and you were wrong. Were you grateful for this person's assertion or correction? Or on some level, did you resent his delight in being right? The fact is none of us likes to be told we're wrong.

What would happen if we opted to listen instead of attempting to be right? People who listen well and take *pleasure in understanding* are respected; people who need to be right are often resented. No one likes a know-it-all.

I'm not suggesting that it's never right to speak your mind. We all have core values and beliefs, and it would be wrong to compromise them. Most of the time, however, what other people say is of little or no infringement on our personal beliefs. We can grant them a pass.

When we defend what doesn't need to be defended, usually it's because our ego is in the way. The need to be right convinces us that we know it all and we alone have the right answer. When we force what we think or believe on others, the effect, even if unintended, is to devalue their point of view. Perhaps we are in the know, but the wise person feels no compulsion to display his knowledge.

The next time you're in an argument or discussion, decide that you will allow the other person the opportunity to be right. Would that decision affect you all that adversely? Not really. In fact, it might actually be freeing. And how would the other person feel? He would have the satisfaction of being right. Why not delight in allowing the other person that pleasure?

If you stop asserting your right to be right and try instead to understand, others will be more at ease and less defensive. Then when something does need to be said, when a point does need to be made, others will be more likely to hear you. They will receive what you say as words of wisdom.

Walking the path of wisdom . . .

1. Can you think of a time recently when you insisted on your own opinion and didn't allow the other person the opportunity to be right?
2. What could you have done differently to give the other person the "last word"?
3. What might happen in your relationships if you decide not to assert your right to be right, especially when it comes to issues that are not core values?

16.

Display Character by Restraining Your Anger

A fool gives full vent to his anger, but a wise man keeps himself under control (Proverbs 29:11, NIV).

In the movie *Falling Down*, the hero (actually an anti-hero), frustrated by the maddening happenings of everyday life, such as being stuck in traffic, goes on a rampage of destruction in attempt to "make things right." But as we all know, angry reactions do not make things right; they usually make matters worse.

We have all reacted in anger and said or done thoughtless or hurtful things. These reactions wound and cause strife. Pillows wet from sobs, sensitive natures seared into silence, longtime friendships damaged or ended—these are but a few of the destructive consequences of unbridled anger. Soon thereafter, we will wish it possible to undo the pain we caused.

Typically, anger arises when we are frustrated by something we want or expect. Then, since we're unable to get the outcome we want, we lose control. When my computer freezes, I'm unable to finish what I want to finish, and in my frustration, I might hit the case or curse the screen. Likewise, when people don't do what I expect, frustration arises and I will probably snap or yell.

How can you bring anger under control?* Change your expectations or desires. For instance, you're stuck in traffic, and naturally you expect to get to work on time—but given the circumstances, that's not going to happen. Instead of slamming your fists into the steering wheel (we've all done it), make a conscious effort to change your thoughts. Deliberately choose a different expectation. Decide to use the unexpected situation to your advantage.

Now that you expect to make the most of the problem, you can act on your new expectation: listen to a game on the radio, make a few phone calls, write out a to-do list, or simply pray. You are now at peace with the situation, and you can deal with being late for work when you get there.

Someone who controls her anger is a person of understanding and discipline. She has learned from her mistakes; she has seen the folly of her outbursts. By regularly checking her expectations and desires, she has trained her mind not to react. Her calm manner douses volatile situations. She brings sensibility to frustrating circumstances and peace to quarrels. Others want to be around her; others admire her. I know you, like me, want to be this kind of person.

Walking the path of wisdom . . .

1. What kinds of situations trigger your anger?
2. What role does frustration play regarding your expectations in these situations?
3. What can you do to control your anger in these situations? How might changing your expectations in a situation help to calm your anger?

NOTES:

* One solution is to possess calmness, a peace and restfulness at the depths of a person's nature. The calm person lives in serenity and strength, unruffled regardless the situation. Instead of reacting in anger, exercise calmness. The free chapter, *The Majesty of Calmness,* will show you the way. Find it among other resources at: www.ThePathofWisdom.com/resources.htm.

17.

View Every Situation in Light of Eternity

Wisdom [eternity] is in view of the discerning person, but the eyes of a fool wander to the ends of the earth (Proverbs 17:24).

The fool searches the earth to find something to gaze upon. Typically, he sets his eyes on his immediate problems. Similarly, much of our thinking is given to our present problems, but this is not wisdom's approach. Wisdom sees outside the present. Wisdom views all situations and matters from an eternal perspective—and so can you.

When we react to a situation, we demonstrate a lack of perspective. We have all done or said things we regret. Perhaps when we look back a week later we wonder: *How could I have acted so rashly? How could I have gotten so out of control?* With the perspective provided by a week or two, we see the real importance or unimportance of a situation, action, or attitude.

Well, why wait two weeks to gain that perspective? You can have it in the present by placing the whole situation in the context of eternity. This is wisdom's viewpoint: "Wisdom has been appointed from eternity, from the beginning, before the world began" (Proverbs 8:23). Wisdom takes the long view.

Someone treats you harshly, dings your car, or steals your wallet. How will you react? You lock your keys in the car, your computer crashes, or you lose that promotion. What will you do? You could focus on the problem, but wisdom offers a different perspective. What will any of this matter a year from now? Not a bit. In the grand scheme, in light of eternity, many problems simply do not matter.

The next time you find yourself "wound up," put your situation into perspective. Pause and take a moment. Ask yourself, "In a hundred years, will this matter? In the light of eternity, is this worth my energy?" Most likely the answer will be "No," and you can handle the situation calmly. Then when you look back two weeks down the road, you will see that you handled the matter like a *discerning person*. In the uncertain moment when you might have reacted wrongly, you took the long view. You kept wisdom and eternity *in view*. You deserve a pat yourself on the back.

Walking the path of wisdom . . .

1. Do you ever get "wound up" over what later seems to be rather insignificant? Why do you think that is?
2. What kind of perspective can a day, week, month, or year provide for those things that frustrate you? How might a long view make a difference in how you see problems and situations?
3. Do you think it would be helpful to ask yourself in the moment, "What will this matter in a week or two?" Why or why not?

18.

Peace of Mind Is Better Than Happiness

All of wisdom's ways are pleasant, and all her paths lead to peace (Proverbs 2:10).

The word *happy* has the same root as the words *happening* or *happenstance*. The root *hap* means by chance or circumstance, which is why happiness is not a solid basis for one's life—it's fleeting, based upon circumstances.

Some people say we should avoid happiness altogether. That's not what I'm saying. I'm suggesting that you avoid the other extreme: making happiness the all-important factor. If you make happiness your ultimate end, it will elude you, and in that moment, you will come face to face with the folly of your pursuit.

When someone makes happiness his life's objective, he comes to believe, usually unwittingly, that everything should go his way, that he should have no difficulties. But life is rarely like this, and the pursuer of happiness is regularly disappointed. He ends up with the very opposite of his pursuit. But it doesn't have to be that way.

There's something more lasting than happiness, something much deeper and richer. Wisdom's path leads to a different sort of "feel good." Wisdom produces contentment and satisfaction, in a word—peace.

When you practice wisdom's way, you put yourself in harmony with God, his creation, and others. Wisdom makes you feel at home with the world, content with self, and at peace with others. We might call this peace of mind. The Hebrews called it *shalom*, which includes peace of mind but encompasses much more. *Shalom* refers to wholeness and well-being. *Shalom* is considerably more lasting and meaningful than happiness.

How do we obtain this peace and pleasantness? The path taken for happiness often includes practices that are not consistent with wisdom. Choose wisdom's ways (which is what this book is about), and she will *lead* you to peace. What's more, when we pursue happiness, we might try to bring about the result we think equals happiness. But wisdom says that we have little control over the outcome of our efforts (Proverbs 16:9). *Shalom* comes when we give up control of having the happy ending.

Wisdom's ways differ from the approaches found on the road to happiness. Instead, wisdom's path leads to a completely different destination. Live by her ways, surrender any efforts to bring about a happy ending, and you will gain the lasting effects of *shalom*—peace and pleasantness in all things.

Walking the path of wisdom . . .

1. What might be some problems with making happiness the main pursuit of a person's life?
2. What do you make of the claim that peace of mind is preferable to happiness? Do you think that *shalom* is a more worthwhile pursuit? Why or why not?
3. What can you do to create more peace and *shalom* in your life and your family?

19.

What Are You Looking for in Others?

Those who do right hate searching for wrong [in others], while the wicked spread the stench of scandal (Proverbs 13:5).

At one time or another, we have all had a dislike for a someone based upon our perceptions. Have you ever said, "I don't like such-and-such about so-and-so"? You may even begin to view the person as all bad and fail to see any good in her. Even if your critical view is accurate, the notion that she is all bad is false.

Sometimes people study character like a proofreader pores over a great poem. The reader might miss the beauty of the poem because he is too busy watching for an inverted comma or a misspelled word. His eye is trained for the imperfections. William George Jordan said it well:

> Men who pride themselves on being shrewd in discovering the weak points, the vanity, the dishonesty, immorality, intrigue, and pettiness of others think they understand character. They know only a part of character. They know only the depths to which some men may sink; they know not the heights to which some men may rise (The Kingship of Self-Control, pg. 27).

The fact of the matter is, there's good in everyone; it just depends what we're looking for. If we're looking for the negative in a person, we're sure to find it, because we all have shortcomings. If we're looking for the positive in someone, we're likely to find it, because we all have strengths.

A critical eye toward someone may cause us to respond to him severely. In turn, he will likely respond to us negatively. Before long, animosity between the two parties becomes the norm.

Let's look at people not with an eye toward severity, but with an eye toward charity. Perhaps there is a reason someone is in someway something we don't like. We know nothing of another's hardships, nothing of the tragedy that may hide behind a forced smile, nothing of the secret worries and cares—all of which leave their mark on a person's demeanor and behavior.

Those who do what is right *hate searching for wrong.* Let's make an intentional effort to look for the positive in others, especially in those we tend to view critically. Our new perspective on this person may actually bring a sweet aroma to the environment or relationship (and isn't that better than *stench*).

Walking the path of wisdom . . .

1. Do you tend to be critical of others? Why do you think that is?
2. Can you think of a time when someone was overly critical without giving you much of a chance? How did this make you feel?
3. What steps can you take to look for the good in others? How would it help to realize that there might be a reason behind someone's unfavorable behavior or attitude?

20.

View the World as a Place of Abundance

With me are riches and honor, enduring wealth and prosperity. My fruit is better than fine gold. What I yield surpasses choice silver (Proverbs 8:18–19, NIV).

Some people think that life plays favorites. They assume that the world (or God) has reserved seats for them in "the nose bleed section" and given others the preferred positions. They think life has spread thorns before them and given others a path covered with rose petals. Such people tend to possess an austere attitude that places limits on the resources and gifts available to them from this world (or God).

Certain less-than-attractive qualities accompany someone with this scarcity mind-set. These people take the credit or the profit for themselves; they are unable to share. They are also incapable of being happy for someone who does well; it means they have lost out. These austere people may even become envious and resentful, and seek to obtain material prosperity by improper means; they think it is owed to them.

We don't have to view the world as a place of haves and have-nots; we can have a prosperity mind-set. *Wealth* and *prosperity* are often understood as material, but wisdom offers a spiritual wealth, or to put it differently—a full life.

In Hebrew wisdom literature, the word *wealth* does not always mean affluence or extravagance, but may simply mean plenty. You see, wisdom is concerned that those who heed her ways* flourish with all that makes for health and security, for good life and peace of mind, which has more to do with plenty than excess. It may be hard to fathom, but plenty actually surpasses *fine gold* and *choice silver*. Anyone who possesses wisdom has plenty and is able to see the world as a place of plenty.

Certain attractive qualities accompany someone with this attitude of plenty. These people freely and readily give and help others on their journey; they have no need to greedily cling to praise or possessions. And when others succeed, they are genuinely happy; they know there's plenty to go around. These abundance people posses wisdom and her enduring prosperity; they have no need to obtain by questionable means.

Some people take a scarcity view of reality, but you can choose a positive perspective—a prosperity mind-set. You'll have a greater appreciation and satisfaction in life, and experience it as wealth and well-being to the fullest degree. Accordingly, you'll be more likely to create the life you desire.

Walking the path of wisdom . . .

1. How do you tend to view the world? Do you have a "scarcity" or "plenty" mentality? How did you come to view the world in that way?
2. What do you think it means to view the world as a place of plenty?
3. How can a person change his or her mind-set to view the world as a place of prosperity?

NOTES:

* We usually think of instruction as concepts or principles, but the ancient Hebrew sages turned the idea of wisdom into a person. This person calls out to humanity, offering gifts more valuable than silver and gold. It would be worthwhile to know who this person is. *Meet the Incarnation of Wisdom* in the free article at: www.ThePathofWisdom.com/resources.htm.

21.

Better Single Than in a Contentious Marriage

It's better to stay on a corner of the rooftop than to share the whole house with a quarrelsome wife [or angry husband] (Proverbs 21:9).

A friend, I'll call him Derrick, has had a difficult marriage. The relationship is better now, but there was a time when he and his wife fought incessantly. On a number of occasions, the fighting was so bad that he spent the night, even days, with friends. Derrick and I took many walks around Washington Park during this time, and he would tell me just how miserable he felt. He wanted out.

As much as I struggle with loneliness, I do not want to be in my friend's situation—a contentious marriage. The sage evidently agrees. It's better to be alone *on a corner of the rooftop* (or in the desert, 21:19) than in a household on eggshells. The roof might be an uncomfortable and lonely place, but at least it's free of hostility.

Some people think marriages are made in heaven, but so are tornados, and I don't want to be in one of those. Some view marriage as the position of blessing and singleness as the less desirable state. Granted, marriage can be a gift, but so can singleness. The single life should not be disdained. Like so many supposedly bad situations, matters could be worse—you could be in a painful marriage.

Singles often cite loneliness as the main reason they want to be married. On the one hand, loneliness is a desert in the soul through which the single person must travel. Traversing this wilderness is not pain free, but it is necessary. You see, in the desert we grow in ways that do not occur in the oasis of comfort and ease. On the other hand, loneliness is *not* a time of abandonment. Rather, loneliness is an opportunity to experience in a new and deeper way the only One who can fill that empty longing. Consider what Blaise Pascal said, that there is a God-shaped void in every person.

Frequently (though not always), the reason for our loneliness revolves around our excessive focus on our own plight. Little acts of love surround us, but whatever attention or love we may have, it is not enough given our hunger for more. We may even blame others for their apparent lack of love, but blaming others only increases the ache within us. We need to focus less on how we lack love and see more of the love around us.

Marriage can be like flies on a screen door: Some are trying to get out, and others are trying to get in. If you are single and feeling lonely, you might think the solution is found in marriage, but marriage has its problems too. Just ask anyone wanting to get out.

Walking the path of wisdom . . .

1. In what ways can singleness be a blessing? In what ways can marriage be a hardship?
2. How can a single person face bravely the difficulty of feeling lonely?
3. How can a person be content in any state, whether married or single?

22.

Simplicity's Rewards Trump Those of Excess

It is better to have little with gratitude toward God than to have great wealth with worry (Proverbs 15:16).

Generally, Epicurus has been used to suggest that people should pursue sensual pleasure, but that's not the whole of his philosophy. Consider his quote: "If you want to make a man happy, do not add to his riches but take away from his desires." A growing number of people agree: to be happy, take things away. Increasingly, people are living with less. They drive less, spend less, eat less, and find that less is more. In other words, they live more simply and actually live better.

By the word *simple*, I mean a clear understanding of life's essentials. Simplicity searches through life's vastness and seizes whatever is indispensable to true living. Similarly, simplicity holds in contempt (to some degree) whatever is not essential to real living. This does not mean we can't have or enjoy possessions, but we will probably view them differently—as less important.

A restless hunger for the nonessentials of life remains the hidden reason for much of the Western world's discontent—*great wealth with worry*. Anyone who sees the worthlessness of the material that constitutes the sum of life for others is at the beginning of simplicity. Any person who wishes to live simply, contrary to the masses, must stake his position as a matter of personal conscience. He will need to adjust his life (and that of his family) to his own ideals.

When suffering or difficult times come upon us, we often return to simple practices long since abandoned. In such times, simple things hold new charm, and we realize that we have been renouncing the very things that are best. But why wait for hardship? Let's begin now to cultivate simplicity in our lives.

It may seem simplistic, but the first step towards simplicity is to get rid of excess. Any attempt to live in harmony with the pursuit of more will destroy simplicity. Accordingly, let us live down the needless things that others live up. Let us reduce our encumbrances and increase our peace of mind.

We create many of our supposed hardships by turning inconsequential matters into matters of importance, and this only adds *worry* to our lives. Simplicity allows us to brush aside the trivial issues and say, "They are only disruptions; they are not the real stuff of life." Simplicity enables us to live by the truly important: simple needs, simple habits, simple manners, and simple words.

Walking the path of wisdom . . .

1. What do you think it means to practice simplicity?
2. What can you do to simplify your life? What part does gratitude have in learning to live more simply?
3. What adjustments are the hardest to make when trying to simplify life for yourself and your family? Write down specific steps you might take this week?

23.

There's More to Listening than Hearing

Now, my children, listen to me: Blessed are they that keep my ways and heed my instruction (Proverbs 8:32–33a).

Listening and obeying go hand in hand. When someone corrects us, we might hear and nod in agreement, but if this is all we do, then we've not truly listened. Listening includes hearing what was said, but it also requires an appropriate action or response.

Jesus of Nazareth, the great wisdom teacher, shared a story about obedience with some children. He said a father went to his first son and told him, "Go out in the fields and work." The son said, "Yes," but then didn't go. So the father went to his second son and said, "Go into the fields and work." The second son said, "No," but then decided to go. The great rabbi asked the children, "Which son did what his father asked?" "The second son," the children replied. The principle of listening and obeying is simple enough for a child to grasp, but putting the concept into practice—that's not so easy.

When we agree with a person, that we need to correct our behavior, we give the impression that we have listened and will carry through on the change. For instance, a former girlfriend raised a number of problems in our relationship, and I failed to make the changes we discussed. She concluded from my failure to "obey" that I didn't take seriously what she had said. She put it this way, "You just don't listen to me."

Often when someone tells us something needs to be done, the toxicity of the environment makes it difficult to accomplish the desired behavior. But if we fail to change in these situations, we will inevitably make the environment more toxic. And ironically, the increase in toxicity will make it even more difficult to comply. By not complying, we actually compound the problem. Toxicity is no excuse. No matter the difficulty, we need to fulfill any agreed upon changes.

We can verbally agree when someone asks for a change, but agreeing is no substitute for actually modifying our behavior. The next time we consent to correction, will we continue in the old behavior or will we truly listen? Only action will prove that we have listened. Additionally, when we act in the expected manner, something else happens. We also reduce the level of toxicity. We may even create a positive environment.

We can hear and agree to act accordingly, but without an accompanying alteration in behavior, we have not truly listened. We have only pretended to listen. Before we can say we have truly listened, we will need to comply.

Walking the path of wisdom . . .

1. What is the connection between listening and complying? Why do we find it so difficult to truly listen?
2. How would a failure to comply create greater toxicity in a relationship or environment?
3. How would following through on agreed upon instruction or correction create a positive environment?

24.

Few Things Pay as Well as Diligence

The despairing person does not roast his game, but the diligent person captures the rare prize (Proverbs 12:27).

When you pursue something with the expectation of doing well or being successful, sometimes failure is the result, and you may become disappointed or discouraged. You may then decide to give up on our pursuit, but before you do, reconsider.

A drawn-out longing or perpetual shortcoming can result in a kind of illness—a loss of morale or hope. But fretting over what no power can restore only lessens a person's faith and allows despair to grow. No doubt your ambition or dream is more difficult than cooking what you catch, but don't cease because of despondency or difficulty. The debris of your failures may yet serve as the building material for greater possibilities.

Okay, you have reconsidered and have decided to give this dream or ambition another *try*. But a friend who says, "I'll *try* to pick you up on time," discloses that he is not fully committed to coming. Your friend's attempt to merely try will not ensure that you get picked up, and your attempt at just *trying* will not suffice to accomplish your ambitions. Instead of just trying, try *until*. Keep on trying *until* you are successful. Be diligent.

Break the shackles of disappointment one chain at a time. Divide your dream or ambition into parts and accomplish the simpler steps. This "baby step" approach will give you the momentum to take on the more difficult tasks and realize your long-held ambition.

But what if, despite your best efforts, you never reach your dream? As hard as that might be, it's even harder to live with regret. If you must traverse the path of failure, you'll have the assurance that you did your best. You can then look back without the pang of regret and courageously face the present, whatever it might be, knowing you could not have made the outcome any different.

When we fail, some may criticize us for our supposed lack of success, but what does the prattling world or obnoxious neighbor who has not seen our efforts know of our shortfall? What others think matters little when we know we have done our best.

Decide today that you, *the diligent person*, will pursue the *rare prize*. Never accept failure as final; raise from the ashes a new fortitude. Great men and women achieved, not because they had the best opportunities, but because they never gave up. Their success awaits you and me—the diligent.

See also entries 20 and 92.

Walking the path of wisdom . . .

1. What do you think of the principle: You gain only what you persistently seek (12:27)? Can you cite examples of this from your own life?
2. Should this principle have any effect on the goals you set or the ambitions you pursue? How?
3. What simple steps can you take today to regain some momentum in the pursuit of your dreams?

25.

Vengeance and Bitterness Hurt Only You

A peaceful heart gives life to the body, but bitterness rots even the bones (Proverbs 14:30).

Michelangelo the sculptor and Raphael the painter both received commissions from the Vatican for works of art. While each worked with a different medium and received high regard, the rivalry and bitter spirit between them was so extreme that whenever they encountered each other, they would not even speak.

It is natural to despise someone who does you an injustice, makes your life miserable, or says terrible things about you. And if your enemy falls, you may even want to rejoice and break out in dancing. But Solomon instructs us *not* to be glad when an enemy stumbles (24:17–18). You see, any joy in an enemy's demise reveals a deep and disturbing problem—the presence of resentment and bitterness. These cancers dwell beneath the surface and rot to the bone, which includes body, mind, and soul.

Bitterness inflicts damage on our bodies. Bitterness ruins a person's appetite, increases tension in the body, or damages the body altogether. A number of medical studies show that physical maladies such as high blood pressure, strokes, and ulcers can be attributed to lingering hostility or hatred. Don't let this be you.

Bitterness wreaks havoc on our minds. When our thoughts dwell on an enemy—what he has done to us, or what we want to do to him—we waste mental energy. Our minds, which produce our best success and represent our finest activity, are led away and rendered useless. Resentment or hatred enslaves our thoughts, and our minds accomplish nothing but obsession.

Bitterness destroys our souls. The person who lets bitterness grow in her heart poisons her judgment, destroys her higher emotions, and diminishes her capacity to love. If her enemy pleads for understanding or forgiveness, she will shut her ears and allow intolerance to harden any sensitivity. Her bitterness harms her more than the object of her hatred. Slowly, she destroys her own soul.

If resentment reigns in us, we make ourselves slaves to the person we detest. Even if this individual lives in another state or is dead, we have placed ourselves under his or her dominion. Why give someone who has wronged us that kind of destructive influence?

There is a better way. If we can be at peace and free from hostility, we will give *life to the body*. Let's reign over ourselves by conquering any element given to resentment. All the wrongs done to us end today; we put them where they belong—in the past.

See also entries 8 and 57.

Walking the path of wisdom . . .

1. What effect does bitterness have on a person?
2. Can you think of someone you resent? How has this bitterness hurt you?
3. How might you conquer resentment towards this person?

26.

Be Concerned with the Less Fortunate

One who despises the poor insults the Creator, but one who is kind to those in need honors his Maker (Proverbs 14:31).

The references to *Maker* and *Creator* in this proverb suggest that rich and poor alike are creatures. Neither one is fully self-reliant; each must depend on their Maker. This commonality among humans as mutually dependent creatures is one of the primary reasons to treat the poor with compassion. We never know when we may find ourselves in the same position of needing assistance. There are some steps we can take to demonstrate in a practical manner our common humanity.

Show genuine empathy. A person who is overwhelmed with the hardships of poverty may be given to discouragement. But if your intention is to "cheer them up," don't be overly cheerful. The best response is genuine empathy. Generally, people are less likely to get down on themselves if they know someone cares.

Don't regard the poor as victims. The poor may be suffering due to forces outside of their control, such as layoffs or inadequate take-home pay, but treating them as victims is less than helpful. A poor person might have fewer options, but that doesn't mean she has no options. Calling the impoverished victims blinds them (and us) to their alternatives.

Break the habit of guilt. There are those who try to place blame on people with money in an attempt to create resentment between the haves and have-nots. Don't fall for it. The fact that others have more is best used as an opportunity to generate hope and not guilt. You don't have to feel guilty for having money. Actually, you're in a good position to help the poor, even to assist them in getting out of poverty.

Encourage business people to offer low-cost options. The lack of decent housing among the poor is a demand seeking a supply and is best met by private industry. If we have the occasion or position, we may issue a challenge to property owners and developers or to banks and venture capitalists to meet the demand. These endeavors would not have to be charitable; there is nothing wrong with making a profit while meeting a need. Encourage conversations on these issues in religious gatherings, boardrooms, or partners' meetings.

All humanity shares a collective insecurity. The same uncertainty of life that compels the wise to make provision for the future should also foster among the wise an awareness for the necessity of charity. After all, we never know when we may find ourselves in a poor person's position and need assistance. We give knowing, at some point, we may have a need.

See also entries 13 and 71.

Walking the path of wisdom . . .

1. What should be your attitude toward the poor? Why?
2. How can you be of assistance or encouragement to the poor? Can you think of other ways in addition to those listed above?
3. Do you know someone less fortunate? What practical steps can you take to help this person?

27.

When Criticism Comes: Accept or Deflect

He who listens to life-giving rebuke will be at home among the wise (Proverbs 15:31, NIV).

This proverb describes rebuke as *life-giving*, but most of us probably feel like correction takes the life right from us, especially if it comes harshly or cruelly. We find criticism to be draining, exhausting, and painful—anything but life-giving. Understandably, we feel we must resist correction.

The typical knee-jerk response to criticism is to get defensive. This reaction, however, has a way of making the person doing the correcting even more insistent. One proverb (17:10) compares resisting correction to receiving a hundred lashes. The more we oppose, the more the lashes come. Wisdom offers two approaches that do not bring as much harm and may even be life-giving.

The first method is to receive the rebuke. Our teacher of wisdom compares accepting correction to obtaining fine gold or jewelry (25:12). Evidently, you may enrich yourself when you receive criticism. You see, for the most part, the motivation behind criticism comes from good intentions. By listening to people who will be honest with you, you increase your capacity to live well, and the rebuke becomes life-giving.

We can receive criticism by identifying what is right (or possibly right) in what the other person is saying and respond with something like:

1. "You may have a point there."
2. "I'm going to seriously consider what you have said."
3. "I may need to make some changes."

The second option is to deflect criticism. Maybe the words are not the words of a friend; maybe the reproof does not come with good intentions; maybe the person is just plain wrong. We should not be quick to assume improper motives or conclude the other person is wrong, but when that is the case, we can simply deflect the criticism. To do this, check your emotions before you speak and say something like:

1. "Thanks for being honest with me."
2. "Thanks for taking the time to share how you feel."
3. "I can see how you might feel that way."

When we resist criticism, we invite even more correction, and this might actually cause us more pain. A life-giving approach would receive or deflect criticism. These simple, subtle, and effective responses will enable us to handle the other person, but more important, they will make us better people. Our attempts to handle correction in life-giving ways will put us *at home among the wise.*

Walking the path of wisdom . . .

1. Think about a time when someone criticized you; how did you react? How could you have reacted differently? How does correction help a person? How might it hurt a person?
2. Are you able to deflect unkind words of criticism, or do you tend to take them to heart? How can you change that response?
3. Why might correction be highly regarded by those who are wise? What has been your experience with correction?

28.

Do Not Neglect Your Friendships

Most people will proclaim their own loyalty, but who can find a trustworthy friend? (Proverbs 20:6)

Some friends are like the man who tried to find a birthday present to ship to an out-of-state friend. He searched all the stores and malls for just the right gift—a cheap one. Eventually, he came upon a beautiful vase at a great price. The only problem? The handle had broken off the vase (thus the price). The clerk offered to wrap the vase, and the man figured his friend would think the vase broke during the shipping. A week after the friend's birthday, the man received a note: "Thank you for the beautiful vase. It was so nice of you to wrap each piece separately."

Undoubtedly, this broken-gift-giver thinks of himself as a good friend and proclaims his *own loyalty*. But we know better. How can we avoid the shortcomings of this man and be that rare commodity—*a trustworthy friend?*

Real friends invest in one another (Proverbs 27:9, 17). No one appreciates a friend who consistently takes without contributing something to the relationship. Relationships can be compared to a bank account. Taking without giving is like making withdrawals without making any deposits. Soon we deplete or overdraw the account, or in this case, we deplete the friendship. We can't expect friends, even longtime friends, to be there for us when it has been a long time since we invested in them.

Real friends support each other (Proverbs 17:17; 18:24). Friends share their joys and bear each other's sorrows. A trustworthy friend offers life-giving support when the weight of life seems too much to bear. When our friends carry heavy burdens, our responsibility and privilege is to lighten their load with an encouraging word or gentle embrace. And we stick with them for the "long haul."

Real friends don't hold grudges against one another (Proverbs 17:9). True friends demonstrate a willingness to overlook offenses. We can choose not to cling to the wrongs friends commit against us. This no grudges approach also means we don't retaliate. For instance, we don't conveniently forget a friend's birthday if he forgets ours. And if we need to make amends with our friend, then we do so—even if he is unwilling to reciprocate.

We are not responsible for our friend's actions, but we are responsible for our own. Regardless of what our friends do or don't do, we can choose to be a rare commodity—the kind of friend who sticks closer than a brother (Proverbs 18:24). This type of trustworthy person is hard to find; fair-weather friends abound. May our friends find in us a loyal and dependable friend.

Walking the path of wisdom . . .

1. How do your friends treat you? How do you treat them? Is there a better way to be a friend?
2. What does a trustworthy friend look like? Can you think of other examples in addition to those above?
3. What can you do this week to support a friend? Is there someone you need to call? Is there a deposit you need to make?

29.

Give Your Spouse Preeminence

For three things the earth is perturbed, . . . for a servant when he reigns, a fool when he has had his fill, [and] a wife when she is unloved, . . . (Proverbs 30:21–23).

Some things are so severe that even the earth itself shakes. When a servant comes to power, he has many grudges to rectify. Hence, he becomes more odious than the previous lord—and the earth trembles. When a fool has his fill, there's nothing left to pacify his empty feelings. Thus, he makes everyone feel his worthlessness—and the earth trembles. When a woman in marriage goes unloved, spite eventually consumes her. As a result, she takes out her pain on other people—and the earth trembles. The result is no different when a man goes unloved—the earth still trembles.

For our purposes, let's focus on the sage's last observation: the unloved spouse. A common occurrence in marriages is that partners like the privileges of matrimony but disdain the obligations. Certain matters—kids, friends, work, or something or someone else—have a way of taking precedence over a spouse. Consequently, the spouse falls to second place or lower. The longer this goes on, the more it festers in the heart of the significant other. He or she then feels more and more insignificant.

A husband and wife should give each other their rightful place of honor. No other earthly being and no other earthly obligation should take the place of prominence reserved for your spouse.

Some spouses might think that if they give their mate priority, they won't get to do the things they enjoy. But the opposite is true. For instance, the more important a wife feels she is to her husband, the more likely she is to encourage him to do the things he enjoys.

What place does your spouse have? Gary Smalley, a well-known marriage and family author, suggests a few questions you can ask your mate regarding the place he or she takes in your life.

1. Do you feel that you are the most important person in my life?
2. Are there any activities that you think are more important to me than you?
3. Are there any specific or special ways that I could better communicate or demonstrate to you just how important you are to me?

When you give your spouse his or her rightful place of honor, you make your marriage (and your life) more pleasant. As one husband put it, "A happy wife makes for a happy life." And a wife could say something similar: "A contented husband makes for a calm marriage." By putting your mate at the top of your world, you can keep your marriage from shaking (not to mention the earth).

Walking the path of wisdom . . .

1. Have you allowed other matters or people to take precedence over your spouse? What are they?
2. We may not know how our mate perceives his or her place. Would the questions above help in gaining a better understanding of the true nature of your relationship?
3. How would giving your mate the proper place of earthly prominence make your life on earth better?

30.

Do Not Make Hasty Promises

A person ensnares himself when he makes rash vows and only later considers how to keep them (Proverbs 20:25).

Making a commitment is costly, requiring the expense of time, energy, and perhaps money. Too many people make promises in the emotion of the moment. Only later do they realize they have entrapped themselves and can't back out unless they go back on their word, which can be just as costly.

The word *vow* in our proverb carries the connotation of *sacred*—a vow or promise is sacred, not to be broken. The wisdom teacher suggests that once a person makes a promise, he is responsible to *keep* the vow. If keeping this promise puts him in a less than desirable position or obligation, then he has ensnared himself. This unenviable position, however, is not sufficient reason to back out of the vow. In fact, if a person develops a habit of breaking promises, others won't trust what he says or promises.

Do you find yourself making unwanted promises? Perhaps you have a hard time saying no. If you have no time for your family, if your relationships are suffering, or if you're constantly stressed, all because you're exhausted from your commitments; then more than likely, you have said yes too many times. You cannot meet every need.

If we tend to overcommit, we need to examine why. What unhealthy need are we trying to satisfy? Some people help others so they can be liked; it's in their nature to please. For other people, being busy makes them feel important or keeps them from facing their inner pain. Whatever the reason, once we know it, we can guard against the compulsion to meet the unhealthy need.

When someone requests your time or service, you don't have to answer right then. Rarely should you make a commitment on the spot. Simply tell the person that you need time to think about it. Get away from the pleading voice and longing expression to consider the expense in time, energy, and resources. Ask your spouse (or family) about it. After all, he or she is usually the one who suffers when you're overextended.

It is better not to vow than to vow and not pay. We do ourselves and others a favor when we carefully *consider* our commitments before, not after, we make them. Then we won't put ourselves in the uncomfortable position of trying to keep or cancel a commitment that we cannot fulfill. As a result, the promises that we do make will likely be kept, and kept with vigor.

Walking the path of wisdom . . .

1. Do you tend to over commit? Are there certain situations in which you tend to say yes too quickly, without thinking it through?
2. Why do you think you have a hard time saying no?
3. What can you do or say in those situations to avoid overcommitting?

31.

Care for All People, Especially Your Enemies

If your enemy is hungry, give him something to eat; if he is thirsty, give him water to drink. In this way, you will heap burning coals on his head (Proverbs 25:21–22).

Our proverb tells us that we should meet the needs of both our friends and our enemies (14:21). Caring for my neighbor or friend, that makes sense, but I'm not so sure about my enemy. Most people, including me, think an enemy deserves condemnation, not compassion.

What are we inclined to do when it comes to an adversary? If we are honest with ourselves, the first thing we want is to get even. But anyone who seeks revenge keeps his wounds open. The typical reaction—to respond in kind when wronged—is not found in *Proverbs*. Instead, we see the opposite injunction: Do not return evil with evil. Wisdom knows that letting go of your hatred is better than the harm you inflect on yourself from resentment.

Often we think the only way to have goodwill with an enemy is if the enemy takes the first step. He should apologize or make amends, not me. But what if you took the first step, not just to apologize but to demonstrate genuine care? Remember, your enemy, whether due to a little incident or a major offense, is like you—a person with needs.

Our proverb compares caring for an enemy to *heaping burning coals on his head*. "Now that's more like it," you say, but this idea is actually a good thing. The imagery comes from an Egyptian penitential ritual in which live coals were placed on a penitent's head as a mark of contrition. The reference is to the pain involved in the penitent's remorse. Similarly, the kindness you show an enemy is so unexpected that it burns his conscience, teaching a lesson no retribution could. Hostility may conquer your enemy, but only compassion will turn his heart.

When an enemy is expecting revenge, he is vulnerable to kindness. Caring for an enemy not only provides for his needs, but in most cases, it also removes his enmity, and he will usually respond with kindness. Even if your enemy doesn't welcome your goodwill or respond favorably, you will have the satisfaction of knowing you did the noble thing.

The proverb charges us with charitable behavior toward those who have wronged us. This means we should avoid indulging our passions of hate and enmity and choose to respond with care and compassion. As difficult as this practice may be, it's healthier for us to show kindness to someone contemptible, and it spares others from our wrath (which would lay the whole world to waste if continually indulged).

See also entry 25.

Walking the path of wisdom . . .

1. What do you think of the charge to care for your enemies?
2. Why do we find it so hard not to respond in kind?
3. How might caring for your enemy turn your enemy to contrition?

32.

Complaining Serves Mostly to Annoy

Pleasant words bring healing like a tree of life, but words of complaint crush the spirit (Proverbs 15:4).

People who tend to complain not only crush their own spirit, but also the morale of others. A change in attitude would not only improve the complainer's view of reality, but also release other people from their destructive and annoying words.

Complainers have a tendency to voice their sense of futility. They know the way they want things, become frustrated that things are not so, and then let their feelings be known. Their problem is this: they focus solely on what is wrong and fail to see what could be.

Complainers wallow and whine. Their irritable attitude goes on and on with no solutions and no intent to change. This perpetual whining may draw others into their misery—"misery loves company." But the more common result is that others become increasingly annoyed and distance themselves.

The first thing for any complainer to decide is this: Do you will to be well? Some people get a weird satisfaction or comfort out of their misery and don't want to change. But for those complainers who want to complain less, there are some things they can do.

One solution to perpetual negativity is to switch from a focus on the problems to thoughts on problem solving. Instead of making sweeping generalizations about your problems, break them down into specifics that you can actually do something about. Then put your creative and positive energy to work on the specifics.* Solve the problem.

Another solution to complaining is this: Make an effort to notice and celebrate what is going right in your life. How often do you accomplish success and milestones without taking notice? This failure to recognize your successes robs you of a more satisfied outlook on life.

A tendency to complain and be negative, perhaps unconsciously, may seek to arouse sympathy, but this type of attitude usually drives people away. Reverse your attitude. Decide that you will bring positive thoughts and creative energy to a difficult or challenging situation. A positive perspective will annoy less people, and others will find it more pleasant to be around you.

Walking the path of wisdom . . .

1. What situations cause you to complain? How would you know if you're complaining or not?
2. Do you think the above suggestions could help a complainer to complain less? Why or why not?
3. Is there a situation you're complaining about? Take a second look at the problem and ask yourself, "Where would I like this to go? And how can I get there?"

NOTES:

* If you let irritating influences get the better of you, you're demonstrating your inferiority to them. One solution is to practice calmness, a peace and serenity in all situations. Instead of complaining, exercise calmness. This free chapter, *The Majesty of Calmness,* taken from the book by the same title can be yours. Visit the resource page: www.ThePathofWisdom.com/resources.htm.

33.

Take the Good in Every Bad Situation

A beautiful sight gladdens the heart, and a good report puts fat on the bones (Proverbs 15:30).

The story of Joseph is one of the great narratives in the Hebrew tradition. Joseph at first appears like the typical spoiled child—the favorite of his father, Jacob, but this made Joseph less than favored by his older brothers (ten in all). Animosity toward Joseph only increased when he foolishly told his bothers of two dreams that placed him in a future position of power and them at his feet. The older brothers subsequently sold the usurping brother into slavery (that'll teach him!), and he eventually landed in a dismal Egyptian prison.

Injustice persistently follows Joseph, but a sudden turn of events—convincing interpretations of Pharaoh's dreams—gets him out of jail and garners him a place of honor in Pharaoh's court. With all of the Near East in a long and severe drought, Joseph, in his new position of power, was able to assist his brothers with grain. They came to Egypt to seek assistance, but they didn't know they were getting it from their long-lost brother.

Joseph tells his brothers, bowed before him, "What you intended for harm; God intended for good—to accomplish what is now being done, the saving of many lives [from drought]" (Genesis 50:20). Evidently, Joseph came to develop a divine perspective, an ability to see the good in what many would consider horrible circumstances.

One way to view life is to see it as a stream of connected events, and we view these events as either negative or positive. Often, negative incidents are negative because that is the value we have ascribed to them. At other times, circumstances are negative because they are truly difficult or tragic. Even so, as was the case with Joseph, we can believe that good can come of the hardship or tragedy. Whether events are labeled negative or are truly distressing, we have the power to determine how we will view the situation—with a divine perspective.

A divine perspective is necessary to see hardship in a positive light or imagine an ultimate good. For our purposes, a divine perspective refers to the ability to step outside of the circumstances and see a *beautiful sight* or hear a *good report* where others see the ugly or hear the negative.

Just like Joseph, we can find the good in any bad situation. All we need is the ability to differentiate ourselves from the circumstances. The more we are caught up in the circumstances, the more likely we are to react emotionally and ascribe negative perceptions. Consciously stepping back from a situation, whether literally or figuratively, not only gives a divine perspective, but also enables us to see and hear in a way that *gladdens the heart.*

See also entry 12.

Walking the path of wisdom . . .

1. Do you tend to ascribe a negative value to what might otherwise be considered a neutral event? Why do you think this is a struggle for you?
2. What do you think it means to have a divine perspective?
3. How might it be beneficial to develop a divine perspective regarding difficult or tragic situations?

34.

Complacency Accomplishes Little but Regret

A little sleep, a little slumber, a little folding of the hands to rest, and poverty will come on you like a bandit,... (Proverbs 24:33–34, NIV).

Those given to complacency (and I'm one of them) seem to think that a *little* doesn't matter—a *little* relaxation, a *little* procrastination, a *little* avoidance of responsibility, a *little* living for the moment. But over time a *little* adds up to a lot. The logical and eventual outcome of living by doing *little* is irreparable loss. While people who are comfortable doing little may not feel regret in the moment, they will face regret when they look back upon the waste of their lives. Perhaps it will be a week, a month, or years later, but later has a way of bringing our lives into better focus.

In addition to thinking a little won't hurt, procrastinators justify their choices with excuses. The listless person sees a metaphorical lion wherever he looks (22:13; 26:13). He is afraid that he will be hurt or come to ruin. Likewise, some people excuse their complacency because they see a "hedge of thorns" at every turn (Proverbs 15:19). They see only the difficulties. These examples illustrate how procrastinators are given to excuses.

The procrastinator also tends to opt out of what the broader culture considers important. He avoids most responsibility with no sense of regret. As a result, he allows himself a weak contentment with whatever his lot may be.

I wonder how many people are like me; they see lions and thorns wherever they turn. When something needed to be done, I often gave undue focus to the potential loss or difficulty. I assumed failure or adversity, and it overwhelmed me. I became comfortable with a life of little responsibility.

Looking back has been a hard lesson. Now I see clearly how doing little has hurt me much. The metaphorical poverty came upon on me *like a bandit.* A perpetual refusal to deal with the matters of life invariably led to some kind of loss. You can avoid this outcome. Choose to rid yourself of excuses and procrastination while you still have time to make the most of the present.*

The wise person knows that complacency is not unusual; it's typical of the person who has made too many excuses and postponements. Taking time to reflect on our tendencies might curtail complacency. Any squander or feelings of emptiness we find in this reflection should serve to move us out of procrastination. Then we can take back what complacency has stolen.

Walking the path of wisdom . . .

1. Has complacency ever been an issue in your life? What are some of the consequences of complacency?
2. Think about why you might be procrastinating. What kind of excuses are you creating?
3. Is there something you've been putting off that you know you should do? How might you start this project or complete what you meant to do?

NOTES:

* Sustaining real or transformative change is difficult. A key reason, other than procrastination, is that unhealthy beliefs govern our actions. *Affirming the Path* will assist you in creating the right inner "framing" for living out wisdom's principles. Visit www.ThePathofWisdom.com/resources.htm.

35.

Invest Your Life Doing What You Love

A longing fulfilled is sweet to the soul, but a fool detests turning from evil (Proverbs 13:19, NIV).

The fool is so committed to the pursuit of evil that nothing deters him. He detests the very thought of turning from his course. This single-mindedness is admirable, even if the pursuit is not. Plenty of people have commendable longings and passions, but they lack the wrongdoer's single-minded devotion to what he loves. In fact, many people spend their lives doing what they can't stand—most notably their careers. Conversely, some people have found personal authentic fulfillment in a livelihood that expresses their *longing*.

In the book *Do What you Love; The Money will Follow*, the author encourages people to pursue their soul's passion. What does your soul long to do? Whatever the passion, even if it's initially done as a hobby, it's the starting point for genuine satisfaction.

For many years, my mom ran her own day care. For years before that, she worked as a day care teacher for someone else. She worked long hours, especially in her own business, and she thoroughly enjoyed it. She didn't make much money, but that didn't matter to her. She loved working with kids; she loved every day of her job. My mom has inspired me to pursue what I love to do.

Many people are concerned with having a certain standard of living, and while they might be making money hand over fist, they are not happy. I don't know about you, but I would rather have little and be happy than have much and be miserable. Yes, we have responsibilities to family and creditors, but to view employment as a means to fulfill these responsibilities is not the best formula for living well (i.e., doing what you love). No material possession compares to the sweet satisfaction of a *longing fulfilled.*

If you pursue your longing, monetary rewards may not immediately follow, but eventually you can expect to make enough for what you need. In the meantime, you may need to continue working and/or advance your studies to keep your dream alive. For instance, an artist who is not proficient enough to sell her work will need to work another job while she is practicing to become a marketable artist.

Many people feel trapped in their jobs and misery is the inevitable consequence. The solution: Make your life count for the very thing your Creator intended. Find a way to do what you love.

Walking the path of wisdom . . .

1. What are you really passionate about?
2. Are you doing what you love? If not, why?
3. What steps can you take to pursue a career that reflects your passion?

36.

Remain Leery When Loaning Money

Do not be among those who put up surety. If you subsequently have no way to pay, you may find your only bed snatched from under you (Proverbs 22:26–27).

The teacher of wisdom warns against providing surety, which may include taking on someone's bills, co-signing a loan, or loaning someone money. With the first two situations, if the debtor fails, the creditor will not go after him, but after you, and will snatch your bed *from under you*. The more common third situation likewise carries the risk of loss. The warning is not a prohibition against helping a neighbor with a loan, but is meant to encourage careful reflection before providing a loan or security.

First, assess your situation as to what you can realistically accomplish. Realize that when loaning money you need to maintain liquidity. If your money or credit becomes tied up elsewhere, and a crisis arises in your life, then the money is not available. Avoid putting yourself in this vulnerable position. The moment you promise more than you can afford, you actually extended the money of others. After all, you will need to go to someone else to cover *your* shortage.

Second, consider whether the potential debtor is responsible with his money. Often, people are in financial predicaments because of poor financial decisions. If you loan them money or provide surety, they are likely to make more unwise decisions. Good counsel with this person might be necessary before extending a loan. For example, you could show them how to live modestly, pay off their debts, or save money. Perhaps you loan the money with the stipulation of accountability to you or someone else. Don't just loan people money, but help them make better decisions and secure a better financial future.

Even a person who is conscientious in the area of providing surety may still find herself in a situation where the right decision is not clear. In this case, it is better *not to give* and be thought selfish than *to give* and later regret the decision as foolish.

A rash loan given to another, and the subsequent loss, seems to have been common in the days of Solomon. And it's common today too. To avoid the misstep of countless other people, we should carefully reflect before providing a loan. When we know we have sufficient means to bolster our brother (sister), when we have determined the person is reliable, and we believe the risk to be reasonable, then so be it. Let us loan to our neighbor or friend.

Walking the path of wisdom . . .

1. What do you think of the suggestion to carefully weigh any decision to loan someone money?
2. Do the suggestions for assessing your situation and the potential debtor make sense to you? Why or why not? What other factors might be good to consider?
3. Do you agree with the statement: "It is better not to give and be thought selfish than to give and later regret the decision as foolish"? Why or why not?

37.

Seek Wise Counsel on Important Decisions

Make decisions by seeking guidance, and if you wage war, then obtain advice (Proverbs 20:18).

The value of this proverb about political governance is obvious. A nation or state without counsel is not likely to succeed, especially in war, but this truth is equally important to self-governance. Wisdom is suspicious of a person's decisions and plans when made in isolation.

Humanity is both individual and corporate, which means, individualism is only half true. Thus, a reliance solely on self for counsel is only half guidance. Ultimately, the decision for one's life lies with the individual, but making important decisions without the input of others is less than safe, and certainly less than wise (Proverbs 15:22).

Only the foolish person remains convinced that he can't make a poor decision. His chief problem is his delusional self-reliance as the only source necessary for guidance. Not surprisingly, he follows his own counsel to eventual ruin. Conversely, the wise person increases his capacity for good decision-making by increasing his counsel. He seeks those who have gone before him, but he also listens to those who have not yet arrived at his station. By gleaning direction from others, he makes his way more sure and the outcome less doubtful.

In one Hebrew story, Naaman, a commander in the Syrian army, a proud man with many military exploits, had a less than glorious problem—a skin disease. A young Israelite servant to Naaman's wife suggested that he should see the prophet Elisha in Samaria (a region in Israel). Naaman consulted with his king and decided to take the servant girl's advice.

Naaman journeyed to Samaria, and upon his arrival, Elisha sent out a servant to instruct him, "Go. Wash seven times in the Jordan River, and you will be healed." Naaman left enraged. He had traveled all this way; he expected to at least see the prophet. Moreover, Syria had two great rivers far superior to the Jordan; why not wash in them?

Naaman's servants suggested that since he had journeyed this great distance, what was 30 miles more to do something so simple? Naaman again took the advice. He traveled to the Jordan, washed seven times and immediately his skin disease cleared. Naaman, a proud man, nonetheless, humbled himself enough to take counsel from others—both great and small.

If Naaman had not taken counsel, any healing would have been in doubt. Similarly for us, counselors can help make our decisions surer. Even if counselors have different views, by considering all sides of a dilemma, we empower ourselves to wisely consider all paths.

Walking the path of wisdom . . .

1. Why are we reluctant to take counsel from others?
2. Has there been a time when you didn't take someone's advice and later regretted it?
3. What decisions do you need to make in the near future? Who can you seek out, great and small, for guidance?

38.

Teach Your Children the Power of Self-Discipline

Have you found honey? Eat only as much as you need, lest you become too full and vomit (Proverbs 25:16).

Nearly every parent has watched a child overeat without any self-control, especially on some kind of sugary confection. And what happens next for the child? Maybe just a stomachache, but it may also turn into a bad night of vomiting. There is a parallel to life in general. If we wish for our children and grandchildren to avoid hurling as an outcome for their lives, we need to teach them self-control.

Throughout this book, I mention my parents and the effect their instruction had on my life. Some proverbs value the father's instruction (Proverbs 15:5), while others hold highly the mother's instruction (Proverbs 3:11–12; 29:15). Each parent's direction is important in providing guidance and setting limits, especially when it comes to self-control.

Completing a task: Teach children not only how to start something but also how to finish it. Children might give up when a task becomes difficult, and too many young people are ready to quit school or a job as soon as they tire of it. They lack the ability to persevere, and this carries over into adulthood.

Delaying gratification: Train a child to wait before he can obtain something he wants. This is important instruction if children are to learn such things as sharing and self-sacrifice. Adults who lack this trait may suffer from poor impulse control and regularly succumb to instant gratification.

Controlling desires: Teach children that they don't have to have everything they desire. So many people in today's permissive and indulgent culture lack the ability to control their desires. All around us are examples of devastated lives because someone gave into their desires without regard for the consequences (or the effect on others).

Fathers and mothers need to tell their children what to do, but equally important, they need to instruct by modeling proper limits. Solomon says, "I have led you [my son] in upright paths" (Proverbs 4:11). The Hebrew word for *path* refers to the furrow made by a wagon. By modeling the way of self-discipline, a father or mother leads a son or daughter in well-worn (proven) paths.

The best gift a parent can give a child is something they probably won't appreciate: limits. A child who learns to rule over his self-serving tendencies learns to make his desires and attitudes his subjects. If as an adult, he does not have a firm command over his unhealthy inclinations, he will indulge them, perhaps even gorge on them, and his life will soon resemble a pool of vomit.

Walking the path of wisdom . . .

1. Why is it that many parents seem to abdicate their responsibility to provide their children with proper limits?
2. How well would the suggestions above work in teaching children self-discipline? What other areas would serve a child well in learning self-discipline?
3. Why is it important for parents to not only teach their children self-discipline but also to model it?

39.

Money Is Not the End-All Be-All

Do not let yourself get weary from pursuing riches; cease from considering it. As soon as you set your eyes on it, it is gone; it will sprout wings and fly away like an eagle into the sky (Proverbs 23:4–5).

A trap that many people fall into when encountering hardships is to think: *If only we had more money, our problems would be solved.* Oddly, such thinking crosses all income levels, whether we're talking $500,000 or $20,000 a year. But pursuing riches to solve problems is foolhardy for one basic reason: Money is transitory. As soon as you set your eyes on it, it is gone. Money is not substantial in any way as a cause or an end. To put it another way, there are many things money simply cannot buy or fix.

Money can't buy happiness. At first, it might seem surprising that so many who have so much can be so unhappy, except when you realize that happiness is not on life's bargaining table—pleasure and possessions, yes, but not happiness. You see, happiness comes from a proper state of mind, not through possessions. Don't fall for money's empty promise of happiness.

Money can't provide purpose. If accumulation is a person's highest purpose, then he reduces his inner self to little more than a safety deposit box. His life closes into a tightly shut fist. He clings to everything he has. True, there are legitimate uses for money, such as providing for your needs, the needs of others, and even for pleasure, but amassing money will not satisfy as an ultimate pursuit. Money is better used as a tool to a nobler purpose.

Money can't provide security. Crime is rampant, and the fear of becoming a victim of crime is just as prevalent. Extra locks, extra dogs, or extra security guards—depending on what one can afford—are attempts to buy safety. Money can give the illusion of security, but the illusion is easily dispelled. Presidents are assassinated and celebrities are gunned down (think of John F. Kennedy and John Lennon), and the common man or woman is no more secure.

Money is handy stuff, and equally true, money is dangerous stuff. How rare is the person who realizes the significance of money and, at the same time, can use it strictly as a servant. If a person allows money to take hold of the reins, "It will drive him until it leaves him utterly winded for anything else" (*Quiet Talks on Personal Problems*, S.D. Gordon, 93).

We might be inclined to think we don't have enough money for it to cause problems, but it is not the amount of money that matters. It's our attitude toward it. If we pursue money as the solution to the ailments of life, then as soon as it is within your grasp, it will *fly away*.

Walking the path of wisdom . . .

1. Why do people fall into the trap of viewing money and/or possessions as some kind of panacea?
2. What should be our attitude toward money? Why? How?
3. What are the dangers and benefits of money? What can money provide; what can't it provide?

40.

Save Seduction for One Person—Your Spouse

Stolen water is sweet, . . . but the simple man [woman] does not know that the dead are found in the seducer's bed (Proverbs 9:17–18).

The Hebrew story of David and Bathsheba illustrates how the sweet but *stolen water* of adultery turns bitter. David's slip across the marriage boundary began rather innocently—a harmless look, but it quickly turned tragic.

King David awoke in the middle of the night, walked out onto his bedroom porch, and gazing across the way, saw a beautiful woman bathing. The sighting of the woman lacked premeditation; nonetheless, it hastened an inquiry, which led to a rendezvous. The rendezvous facilitated a touch, the touch aided a kiss, and the kiss precipitated an adulterous slide. Finally, the adultery wrought an infamous tragedy, which included the murder of Bathsheba's husband.

Unfortunately, so many others repeat David's failure on a regular basis with only minor variations. Lonely women go looking for more than their tired husbands can give them; lustful husbands go searching for something more than their wives can offer. The outcome goes unchanged. To passionately and intimately give yourself to someone who has made no vow and has no commitment is madness and ruin (a metaphorical death).

This tragedy need not be your own. Make sure no seductive words puncture the place of your emotions. Protect your heart. Make sure no lustful thought enters the realm of your imagination. Guard your mind. Make sure no sexual image enters the lens of your soul. Cover your eyes.

Save your heart, mind, and soul from harm. We cannot dwell on lustful thoughts and expect to be impervious to their sway. We cannot bend the ear to someone whispering sweet nothings and expect to resist the swooning. We cannot gaze upon the physical allure of another and expect to avoid longing. The venerable Job made a covenant with his eyes, that he would not look lustfully on a woman (Proverbs 31:1). In like fashion, let us make a covenant not to lust, a covenant not only for our eyes but for our hearts and minds too.

Save seduction for one person—your spouse. Let there be passion, but let it be in the marriage bed. Solomon instructs husbands, "As a loving deer and a graceful doe, let your wife's breasts satisfy you at all times" (Proverbs 5:19). I'm not sure how to rephrase this verse for wives, but with either partner, the meaning is this: Allow yourself to be enraptured solely by your spouse. Love one another sexually, and only one another sexually, and you will save yourselves from the certain metaphorical (and perhaps literal) death of a seducer's bed.

See also entry 70.

Walking the path of wisdom . . .

1. Why do people today seem to take crossing the marriage boundary lightly? What consequences might there be for crossing over into infidelity?
2. How might making a covenant with one's eyes, heart, and mind make a difference?
3. Protect your heart. Guard your mind. Cover your eyes. What are some practical approaches to living out these "on guard" suggestions?

41.

Nice Guys (or Gals) Don't Always Finish Last

A person given to wrong earns an empty wage, but he that sows what is right reaps a true reward (Proverbs 11:18).

One of the best reasons to choose the path of wisdom is this: it's in your best interest. Now you might ask, "What do I get by taking the wise course?" The question is not unexpected (the desire for gain is as old as humanity), but the answer may come as a surprise.

Proverbs suggests there are two ways or paths for life: wisdom's way and the wrong way. The two ways have different outcomes: One *earns an empty wage* while the other *reaps a true reward*. What we *sow* gives us an idea of what we will *reap*. This is called the law of recompense.

The law of recompense is a natural law. That is, it describes the way things are. "Hold on," you say, "things rarely go this way." You make a valid point. We can all identify instances when someone did something good (perhaps you), and the good was overlooked. Likewise, we can all point to people who have gotten gain by questionable means. This outcome may prompt the cynics to say, "Nice guys [or gals] always finish last."

The problem could be that we expect our return to be tangible, obvious, or measurable, such as monetary compensation, material possessions, or the applause of men, but rewards such as peace of mind, satisfaction, or self-respect cannot be placed on a scale or received in an ovation. They are ultimately more rewarding than possessions or social status; they are true rewards.

Typically, when we speak of gain, we are thinking materially, and while *Proverbs* does suggest that we might obtain material rewards by following wisdom's ways, it is not guaranteed. Material rewards may be coming, but if they come, they will come in their season. We must keep in mind that the more visible fruits take time to mature. Wisdom's ultimate objective, however, is not to make you "well off" but to enable you to enjoy life and relationships. I ask you, what good are material possessions if you lack the capacity to enjoy them? The ability to enjoy life, this is a true reward.

You might say we are oblivious to the blessings bestowed upon us from doing right. Instead of looking outward at the measurable, we must look inward to the immeasurable. There we will find our harvest: the contentment, joy, and satisfaction that comes in doing right and living well.

Walking the path of wisdom . . .

1. Do you agree with the statement: "Nice guys [or gals] always finish last"? Why or why not?
2. Can you think of a time when you (or another) got what you deserved—bad or good? Is it generally true that you reap good for sowing good? Why or why not?
3. What are some possible reasons for someone not reaping what they have sown, especially when it comes to sowing and reaping good?

42.

A Kind and Genuine Word Gets Results

Pleasant words are like honeycomb, health to the bones and sweetness to the soul (Proverbs 16:24).

Since our words plant ideas in the minds of others, the fruit of our words can be good or disastrous. The proverb alludes to some possible positive results from the use of our words. *Pleasant* words are *like honeycomb*, offering kindness, and their sweetness benefits the hearer in both body and soul.

Most people will do anything for someone who encourages their dreams, allays their fears, or bolsters their failures. We can be one of these admired people who upholds others by mere words. But given the power of words, we must be careful not to use them to manipulate people. Instead, we should offer words genuinely and for the benefit of others.

Encourage their dreams. Many people do not have a person who believes in them and their dreams. A person who is unable to be her best, beaten down by the never-ending voices, "You'll never amount to anything," needs inspiring words. Your supportive words may bring hope, warmth, and a glow to an otherwise bleak outlook. Because of you and your words, she will dream again.

Allay their fears. We tell people not to be afraid and expect *that* to do the trick. But when someone hears something like, "There's no reason to be afraid," the words sound empty. Conversely, people who actually attempt to alleviate the fear are more helpful. These encouraging people use their words powerfully; they present evidence, tell stories, and verbalize their support. Their words imbue the fearful person with courage; their words ring true.

Bolster their failures. We all make mistakes or fail, but some people find it more debilitating than others. We could manipulatively tell them that they are not responsible for their mistakes, or we could encourage them. If we help others bravely face their collapse (by call, card, prayer, etc.), we may become to them like the stimulating breath of spring. Let us be the voice of hope to those who have lost there confidence, and there may be no limit to their heights or their gratitude.

Every person has an aura about him that affects the people around him, and this is never more obvious than when one opens his mouth. With words, he can spread strife like a scorching fire or kindness like a soothing balm. Words can, in a moment, focus all our latent disgust or release all our hidden hope. Words can be bitter like vinegar or sweet like honeycomb. May our words always be sweet—kind and genuine.

See also entry 64.

Walking the path of wisdom . . .

1. Are your words most often bitter or sweet? What could you do to make your words less bitter and more sweet?
2. Do your words truly have a powerful effect on people? Why or why not?
3. What do you think will happen when you provide uplifting words to those discouraged about their dreams, gripped by their fears, or distraught over their failures?

43.

Confession Is Good for the Soul

The person who conceals his wrongs does not prosper, but whoever confesses and forsakes his erroneous ways will find mercy (Proverbs 28:13).

Most of us are inclined to conceal our wrongs. Why? Maybe we can't bear to reveal our shortcomings to flawless people. I can relate. I occasionally compare myself to put-together people, and as a result, feel inferior and hide my true self. Similarly, maybe we wish to maintain an appearance of having it together. Again, I can relate. I would prefer to manifest a flawless persona, and if I admit my shortcomings, it removes the thin veil of perfection. In either case, we remain in bondage to our wrongs and trapped in guilt.

One solution to the tendency to conceal our wrongs is to give and receive confession. Giving confession includes four things: examination of one's self, sorrow for any wrong discovered, admission of the fault to a mature person, and turning from the wrongdoing. Receiving confession involves only one thing: soul-searching.

Let's look at the process of giving confession. First, examine yourself. Take time to reflect and be specific about what wrongs come to mind. Perhaps write them down. Second, come to an inner place of sorrow. Sorrow refers to a sense of regret and sadness over your wrongs. But be careful. Don't overly scrutinize yourself. Otherwise, your sorrow could result in perpetual self-condemnation. And you're not doing this to berate yourself. Next, confess your shortcomings to someone with the maturity and empathy to extend grace without dismissing the wrong. Last, turn from and *forsake* the shortcoming. In other words, resolve to set a different course in your behavior or attitude.

To receive confession, that is, to hear someone's confession, involves one thing (no, you don't have to become a priest): the ability to search yourself and see your own penchant for wrongdoing. By reminding yourself of your own *erroneous ways*, you avoid the common inclination to feel superior when someone else admits his faults.

When we give and receive confession, we serve a dual role similar to that of the ancient Hebrew priests. Through offerings and rituals, the priests would confess to God the sins of the people, and they would in turn extend to the people the *mercy* of God. While we don't have the special grace of a priest, we are made in the image of God and can represent the face of the divine to another person. When someone confesses to us, we function as God's servant and receive the confession. When we confess to another, she functions as God's servant and extends mercy to us.

When we conceal our wrongs, we cease to *prosper*. When we confess, we are set free from bondage to guilt and self-condemnation. In giving and receiving confession, we experience freedom and discover God's mercy.

Walking the path of wisdom . . .

1. Why do we find it difficult to confess our shortcomings to others? And what about receiving someone's confession? Is that any easier?
2. Is there something you need to confess? Who will you go to? Make plans to talk to the person.
3. What actions do you need to take to forsake this wrong?

44.

Be Slow to Speak Your Opinion

A fool finds no pleasure in understanding, but delights in airing his own opinions (Proverbs 18:2, NIV).

Often in conversation, we are not truly listening to what the other person is saying. Rather, we are anxiously waiting for an opening to speak our own mind. The result is misunderstanding at best and hostility at worst. Given this tendency to verbal sparring, it's no wonder people are often annoyed and irritated with each other.

The sages of wisdom warn us, "Do not go out hastily to argue your case" (25:8). If we "go out hastily," we are acting in an uncontrolled manner—too defensive, too argumentative. We display a compulsion to interject; we can't seem to resist.

Speaking out of turn is an error based in pride. We are convinced that what we have to say is more important or accurate. However, when we interrupt someone, it ruins our credibility and makes our point less effective. A person who interrupts is soon treated like a fool.

Imagine a conversation where you're looking off to the side of a person and focusing on the wall behind her. How much of a connection are you going to make with that person? Not much, which is exactly what happens when we focus on our own opinion in a conversation. We are looking past the person, past everything that is most important to her. Consequently, there is little chance of getting her to see our position. Clearly, interjecting our opinion accomplishes the opposite of what we intend.

Our content may be fine, but that won't matter if our timing is off. Let's wait for the appropriate time—when the other person is finished—to share our thoughts. Let's watch for cues and learn timing in speech, like when an actor waits for cues before giving his lines.

The solution to airing our opinions is to take *pleasure in understanding*. Let's think on what the other person is saying and look for what might be right and accurate in their position. Let's share with the person how we agree and only then point out the differences. This will make us more attentive and less combative.

Taking pleasure in understanding will have a huge impact on your relationships. Others will view you as less contentious, and you'll be amazed at how many people actually react more softly toward you. You may be one of the few people who truly listens to the views of others; this will earn you respect and in turn provide you with a greater audience for your own views.

Walking the path of wisdom . . .

1. Do you find that you have a tendency to speak your mind without regard for what the other person is saying? Why do you think you do that?
2. What can you do to be a person who hears the views of others before sharing your own?
3. How would being a person who truly hears the views of others make a difference in your relationships?

45.

Flattery Causes Stumbling Not Smoothing

Anyone who flatters his neighbor also spreads a net for his feet (Proverbs 29:5).

We can all think of instances when flattery has been effective. Many a career has been advanced by it (brownnosing, as some people call it). But flattery, the art of making someone feel good in order to manipulate them, does not always work. The reality is this: Flattery may actually become a snare or net set for the flatterer or his neighbor.

The Hebrew word for *flattery* means to *make smooth*. Undoubtedly, flattery can work to "smooth out" any number of awkward social situations or make difficult people more tolerable in the present, but wisdom, as always, considers the long-term effects. If we smooth talk a neighbor, friend, or family member, instead of offering her correction or direction, we may actually set a net for her to stumble over, particularly when she repeats the behavior.

Does this mean that we should never praise or encourage family, friends, and others? To the contrary, according to wisdom, an encouraging or uplifting word has its place, but praise can exceed the bounds of truth and appropriateness, and extravagant or repeated praise can come off as insincere. When a person loads up on commending others, they may regard him with suspicion, perhaps even with disgust. Consequently, the flatterer unwittingly ensnares himself.

We can avoid the snare by refusing to use flattery on others. The key is to have the right perspective regarding what matters. First, in regard to attaining some end, something is not worth having if we must manipulate someone to get it. Second, in regard to determining what is valuable, given how it was acquired, anything the flatterer gains is small and insignificant, even if it appears to be great. Third, in regard to deciding what is meaningful, a thousand fair words do not mean nearly as much as a simple, fulfilled promise. When our perspective is right in these key areas, we can avoid flatteries temptations.

We can also elude the snare by disregarding flattery offered by others. The wise person is not easily swayed by exaggerated praise. When you know you do not possess the loveliness described, when you know that what is said is not truly meant, you, the perceptive person, will not be persuaded by the empty words. You have no need to have your ego stroked; the trap does not ensnare you.

Flattery comes easily, costing only the expense of breath, but it just as easily brings detrimental results. When you excessively praise others or otherwise manipulate them with smooth words, you spread *a net for* yourself and them. Avoid giving flattery, and avoid receiving it—either way you'll avoid flattery's entanglements.

Walking the path of wisdom . . .

1. What is wrong with flattery?
2. How does our understanding or perspective on what truly matters affect whether we use flattery?
3. Do you find yourself flattering people to gain their approval? What might you do instead? Conversely, can you tell when someone is flattering you, and can you avoid falling into the trap?

46.

Patience Is More Effective Than Power

The person not given to rash reactions is better than the mighty; the one who rules his spirit is better than he who captures a city (Proverbs 16: 32).

When it comes to problems and conflicts, some people consider it necessary to set things right or get matters off their chest. Yet they are utterly oblivious to any harm done by their rashness. Our proverb points us to a better way, a way hidden from those given to verbal or attitudinal might.

Not long after God had miraculously delivered the Israelites from Egypt, they came to the city of Jericho, a great ancient city, but according to the even greater Hebrew God, Jericho had to fall. The city, however, presented a problem for the Israelites. The massive walls were several yards thick, and the people within the walls lay in waiting.

The Hebrew God offered a solution: March around Jericho daily for seven days. On the seventh day, march around the city seven times with the priests blowing their trumpets. On the last long blast, the entire army should give a loud shout. The Israelites did as instructed, and amazingly, the walls tumbled down.

Like the strange strategy at Jericho, wisdom suggests an unusual battle plan: patience and forbearance. While this strategy is contrary to the norm, it has a way of bringing down walls, walls erected not with stone, but with hard feelings.

Sometimes harmful emotions well up within my spirit, and when I sense this inner swell, it's a cue to guard against any reaction and gain victory over the intensifying feelings. Instead of reacting, the self-aware person subdues his emotions before they get out of control. To accomplish this, he will need to learn and eventually possess patience and forbearance.

The virtues of patience and forbearance have the power to overlook offenses.* Through patience we can bear any annoyance, such as provocation, misfortune, or pain. In forbearance, we refrain from enforcing anything we are due, such as a debt, a right, or an obligation. These virtues possess the ability to pacify contentions and bring about peace (Proverbs 15:18).

A person who captures a city is powerful indeed, and a person of political influence is mighty as well. However, we can outdo the powerful and mighty, not with greater strength, but with something completely unexpected—patience and forbearance. Of all the virtues, none has the same power to make one stronger or to persuade others. The possessor of these virtues is truly mighty.

See also entries 7, 10, 16, 42, and 57.

Walking the path of wisdom . . .

1. How is it possible for patience and forbearance to be positions of strength?
2. What are the similarities and differences between patience and forbearance?
3. How can you gain the victory in times when your patience or forbearance wanes?

NOTES:

* Calmness is a companion virtue to patience and forbearance and has similar power to bear wrongs and endure aggravation. The calm person is unruffled by wrongs and relaxed in the midst of frustration. Find *The Majesty of Calmness* free at: www.ThePathofWisdom.com/resources.htm.

47.

Let Not Your Heart Be Troubled—Stop Worrying

All the days of the inwardly oppressed are wretched, but anyone with a cheerful heart has a continual feast (Proverbs 15:15).

When troubled thoughts and concerns make themselves known all day, every moment and every hour, above all other thoughts, we know then that we are *inwardly oppressed* with worry and anxiety. Worry makes one's days *wretched.*

There are two reasons why a person should not worry. First, because she *cannot* prevent the result she fears. In this case, she needs all her mental and emotional faculties to sustain her strength and bravely face the difficult situation. Second, because she *can* prevent the result she fears. In this situation, worry only hinders her progress and dissipates needed energy for the difficult occasion.

To cure worry, a person must become more self-aware.* He must intentionally put into practice thoughts, attitudes, and actions that give less attention to the uncontrollable past or future, and more attention to a peaceful and cheerful condition in the present.

Stop pleasing others. Living for the approval of others can become a nagging source of anxiety and frustration. If you please one person or group, another person or group will invariably be displeased. You can't control what others think; you can't please everyone. Not even God can please everyone. If people will disapprove of the Almighty, then they also will disapprove of you.

Practice gratitude. Typically, gratitude is one of the first things to go when we're worried. When we focus on being grateful, we're not fretting over what went wrong or over what might go wrong. And in turn, we're less anxious. A simple exercise is to think on someone for whom we are thankful. This usually brings to mind other people and, in turn, leads to things for which we're grateful, such as health, possessions, career, etc.

Welcome assistance. A word for perfectionists (and I'm one of them): You may be the cause of your own worry. Perfectionists are masters of their own universe. They feel they must do everything themselves if it's to be done right, but others are equally capable. We can cheerfully allow others to help us. Letting go of doing everything will mean less to stress over.

A person has no right to waste his own energy, weakening his power and influence with worry, since he has responsibilities to himself, his family, and society. If a person foregoes worry, day by day he will *feast* on living, with no need to fear and no need to regret.

Walking the path of wisdom . . .

1. How does worry and anxiety come to be such a prominent influence in people's lives?
2. Would you agree with the two reasons not to worry? Why? Why not? Are there other reasons to avoid worry?
3. What do you think of the suggestions for addressing the problem of worry? Can you think of other ways to eliminate worry from your life?

NOTES:

* When you fret over the worries and cares of the day, and they wear upon you, choose to be calm. Crown yourself with calmness and quiet your worry. From the book, *The Majesty of Calmness,* get the chapter with the same title for free at: www.ThePathofWisdom.com/resources.htm.

48.

The Often Overlooked Benefits of Poverty

A person of wealth may be wise in his own eyes, but the discernment of the poor person sees right through him (Proverbs 28:11).

Some things are better than wealth and more valuable than possessions, and a *poor* person with *discernment* knows this. Poverty and struggle can be hard and bitter, especially given the daily hand-to-hand battle with fate, but a poor person may likewise be empowered with moral fortitude and contentment. Without dismissing the hardships, the Hebrew sages suggest some advantages for those with less.

The poor tend to live with less anxiety (Proverbs 13:8). Accumulation adds to the stress of life. The rich may be enslaved by worry over what they possess, but the poor person has less over which to stress. He lives with less fear and anxiety. After all, if you don't have anything, it can't be broken and it can't be stolen. As the saying goes, "Poor people fear no thieves."

The poor tend to live in greater awareness of temptation (Proverbs 28:6). The temptations of life come unmasked for the poor. For instance, what some among the wealthy might call "financing" the poor see plainly as stealing. Certain temptations such as greed, superiority, and indifference may come hidden to the wealthy or perhaps mistaken as good, and some wealthy individuals may unwittingly succumb to temptation's subtle allure.

The poor tend to have truer relationships (Proverbs 28:20). Wealth may replace true companionship. A rich person never knows for sure why others are with him. Are they with him for his money? Conversely, no one wants what the poor man has—except his company. Accordingly, the poor person knows the sweetness of true friendships and loyal family, and he can live happily knowing each day is consecrated with lasting relationships.

The poor tend to have contentment and satisfaction (Proverbs 30:8–9). Why does it often seem that those with little are happier or more appreciative than those who have much? Could it be that wealth is the condition of the person who has filled himself with what really matters? Things that cannot be weighed, counted, or measured hold higher value, and ironically, those who have much may lack what is greater.

Those with wealth may look upon their condition as better or superior—*wise in their own eyes*—but some people who have little know they actually have more. A discerning person understands that the truly wealthy are those whose lives are enriched, not with money, but with truer relationships and a fuller satisfaction.

See also entries 9 and 59.

Walking the path of wisdom . . .

1. What do you make of the above benefits to being poor? Agree or disagree? Why?
2. Do you know someone poor who is happier than other people who have more money? Do you know any wealthy people who appear to feel superior to others?
3. What do you make of the explanation about the "truly wealthy"? Agree or disagree? How can you become truly wealthy whether you have much or little?

49.

Do Not Abuse Your Position

There are three things stately in their march, four which are splendid in their movement: the lion, which is great among the beast, and does not retreat from any creature, likewise the prancing stallion and the strutting buck goat, and the king when his army is with him (Proverbs 30:29–31).

The sage Agur draws our attention to the cavalcade march of several creatures: the lion, fearless and proud as he saunters, not retreating from any animal; the prancing stallion and strutting buck goat, both the head of their herds, guiding and protecting; and the king, strong and secure when he is with his army.

We can derive many practical lessons from the grand movements of these four, but for our purposes, we will take them as a metaphor on the proper use of authority. The lion, the stallion, the buck goat, and the king must each lead their respective broods wisely and effectively, lest they or theirs meet with harm.

The wise person in a position of power or authority should imitate the stately qualities of the creatures mentioned here. He should be fearless like the lion, pursuing what is right. He should be a guide like the buck goat, leading others down the proper path. He should be protective like the stallion, always alert to any encroaching danger.

When we come to the king, we see that any position of influence can bring immeasurable good or irreparable harm. A king with his army by him is immensely powerful, and he keeps his army faithful by properly and effectively using his position of authority. If he should become abusive to his army or a tyrant to his people, the army will rise up against him. It's in everyone's best interest that the king's power be used for benevolent ends. Likewise, a wise person uses his authority benevolently.

Men and women of weak character cannot bear positions of power without burdening others with the weight of their position. When unprincipled or mean-spirited people advance, it is the ruin of those beneath them. People in positions of authority, who are also weak in character, show themselves not only to be fools but also to be tyrants.

Anyone in authority is nothing greater or more than the rest of humanity; they simply hold a different position. Those who abuse their power might pounce on others, but they actually ambush their own lives, like a king with his army *against* him. Any person in a position of trust or authority (parents, employers, elected officials, etc.) ought to practice proper authority, like a king with his army *by* him. Let us use our authority in a stately manner, one that brings honor to the position and good to those we oversee.

Walking the path of wisdom . . .

1. What can you learn about the use of authority from the three creatures and the king?
2. Have you been under someone who misused their authority? Under someone who used their authority rightly? How were people under authority affected, depending on the type of authority used?
3. Have you been in positions of authority? Did you find it difficult to use your authority in a constructive manner? Why or why not?

50.

Avoid Zealousness Apart From Knowledge

It is not good to have zeal without knowledge, nor to be hasty and miss the way (Proverbs 19:2, NIV).

A group of people were shown a large poster board with a small black dot in the middle, and they had to answer the question, "What do you see?" The vast majority responded, "A black dot." The person conducting the informal survey then pointed out that the white space was more than 50 times larger than the black dot. Zealousness can have the same effect: We zero in on a point, a dot, and miss the white space—the alternatives, the options, or the differing points of view.

A zealous person might speak or act in haste, but a wise person is characterized by reflection. "The mind of the prudent acquires knowledge, and the ear of the wise seeks knowledge" (Proverbs 18:15). This proverb presents a picture of a person with his ears open, listening, perpetually acquiring more knowledge.

The devotional writer Ken Gire recommends putting *knowledge* ahead of *zeal*. His three-fold approach suggests that we read, reflect, and then respond. The word "read" refers to asking questions of ourselves, the situation, or the other person. Instead of reacting, we take a moment to gain more information. With this new information, we can reflect, that is, weigh and consider what is transpiring in us, the other person, or the situation. After this assessment, we can then choose an appropriate response.

If we hold to a particular position or belief, and assume it to be the only way to think, then we'll probably defend it zealously. During my tenure as an adjunct professor, I taught a course in systematic theology. In that class, my zeal for my particular position on salvation blinded me to how I was presenting the material, unwittingly demeaning students of an alternative view. I have since become more aware that the full truth is always beyond me, that I cannot see and know all things (imagine that). Accordingly, I now teach in a way that allows me to respond better to my students and their varying positions.

When a situation fosters strong feelings, we might react in our zeal, but the joy of the wise is to provide a fitting response (Proverbs 15:23). This does not mean that we abandon what we consider important. There is a place in wisdom for passionate outrage, but the initial step should be to gain *knowledge*—read and reflect. Then we can respond with zeal if appropriate.

Walking the path of wisdom . . .

1. Are there some areas in which you tend to be overly zealous?
2. Do you think that you're able to balance zeal with a need to be "quick to hear, slow to speak, and slow to anger"?
3. What do you think of the three-fold approach to acquiring knowledge before reacting?

51.

Make Reparations Whenever Possible

Fools mock at making amends for wrongs, but goodwill is found among those who make things right (Proverbs 14:9).

Most of us have made mistakes in our relationships and hurt others. When we wrong someone, some people (like me) spend hours chiding themselves over the mistake, but this new error of self-flagellation has no power to correct the original wrong. This bemoaning or regretting behavior is wasted energy, and it accomplishes nothing beneficial for the offender or the injured.

When we commit wrongs against others, wise people, instead of denouncing themselves, seek to make amends. If we can think of anyone whose day we sullied by our selfishness, whose burden increased because of our unkindness, or whose trust waned due to our cruelty, then let us admit the wrong and make things right—if possible.

Generally, you can seek amends with most people right away. But when a serious wound is fresh, when resentments need time to heal, or when one or more parties is given to anger, then you may want to allow some time to pass.

If weeks, months, or years later a wrong comes to our realization, we might be inclined to let reparation "go by the wayside." But people are rarely offended when we ask them to accept payment on an old debt. The exception is when contacting the injured party would cause more injury to self or others. Similarly, you should avoid contact with someone if it would open doors that should remain closed.

Perhaps there are circumstances where "touching base" is not possible. You may have lost track of someone, she may be too ill to receive visitors, or she may be deceased. In that case, set up an empty chair, imagine the individual sitting there, and have a conversation with her. You could also make amends through writing a letter—never to be sent. And if the someone is deceased, you could make a graveside visit to talk with the memory of the person.

The proverb says that we find goodwill when making amends, and while this is usually the case, it is not always so. We need to accept that reparation goes one direction. We cannot expect or require the other person to forgive or reciprocate (though it's natural to desire it).

Only the fool mocks at making amends. Seek to make things right with people, and you will probably foster goodwill. But if others do not reciprocate, you'll have peace in knowing you did what is best for your well-being.

See also entry 8.

Walking the path of wisdom . . .

1. Is there someone you have wronged with whom you haven't made amends? What steps will you take to make amends with this person?
2. What can we do when someone doesn't accept our apology or extend forgiveness? How should we handle this scenario?
3. What can you do to regularly make amends with people rather than ignoring offenses?

52.

The Simplest Explanation Is Usually the Best

Like apples of gold in a setting of silver are words spoken in the appropriate circumstance (Proverbs 25:11).

This proverb suggests the value of good taste and good sense in the use of our words. Words that shine with simplicity's brilliance are *like apples of gold in a setting of silver.* By simplifying our explanations, we can make our speech more appropriate to a situation. But because of a compulsion to explain or defend ourselves, we may find it difficult to limit our words.

At times, we might think it necessary to clear our conscience. But if we say too much, we might say something better left unknown. Then we may accomplish the opposite of what we intend. We end up offending someone or causing even more injury. Reticence in speech may save us and others from embarrassment or unintended injury.

Other times, we may feel obligated to share our knowledge, even when we have no real knowledge to share. But there's nothing wrong with admitting ignorance. And if we do know, the truly knowledgeable person does not flaunt his learning; he uses discretion. The sage makes the point, with a bit of irony, that even a fool can appear wise if he says little (Proverbs 17:28).

Still other times, we may be concerned about what others think and use words to influence their perceptions. Simple speech frees us from this burden of self-justification (Proverbs 25:15). For instance, someone rebuked me in a recent meeting, and immediately I felt a compulsion rising in me to defend myself. But I checked my urge to respond. When I was eventually asked for a reply, I kept my response short and seasoned with grace.

To speak more simply and appropriately in a situation, practice the discipline of restraint. In a world that indulges in noise and clamor, speaking less is just that—a discipline. Practicing restraint does not mean that we refrain from speaking for a predetermined period of time, but that we learn to speak with moderation, pausing or refraining as necessary. If we don't speak when we ought, we miss the mark. If we do speak when we ought not, we miss it again.

Our speech can be our shame or our glory, depending on the suitability of our words. Our communication with others can be more appropriate if we employ simplicity and the discipline of restraint. When we learn to choose our words carefully—*apples of gold*, then others will respect what we say when we do speak.

Walking the path of wisdom . . .

1. Why do people find it difficult to limit their speech to what is appropriate for a situation?
2. How might it be beneficial to you and others to limit what you say when clearing your conscience, sharing what you know, or talking about yourself?
3. Do you think the suggestion to practice the discipline of restraint could be useful in using appropriate speech? Why or why not?

53.

There Is a Proper Time for Everything

As the north wind blows away the rain clouds, so an angry countenance drives away a backbiting tongue (Proverbs 25:23).

If we generalize this proverb, we learn there is a time for everything. For instance, a gentle loving presence is always appreciated, but at times a more severe response—*an angry countenance*—may be necessary. Additionally, just as a storm serves a timely and beneficial purpose, one that sunshine cannot provide, so a genuine frown is as useful as the sweetest smile.

Another work of Hebrew wisdom, *Ecclesiastes*, also addressed this issue of timeliness: "To everything there is a season; a time for every purpose under heaven" (3:1). Innumerable forces are at work in our lives. Some we control, some we don't, but each comes in its season, and opens or blossoms—beautiful in its time.

At one point in my life, I was engaged and my fiancée ended the relationship. The end of this relationship plunged me into despair. A mentor suggested that I see this less-than-desirable season as a time of exile.

Around 500 B.C., the Babylonians brutally defeated Israel's southern kingdom. They took many Hebrews with them to the region of Chaldea. These Israelites had no choice but to live in Chaldea in exile. They would eventually be restored to Jerusalem, but in the meantime, they had something to learn. Likewise, I would one day be restored to hope, but during my unpleasant and difficult exile, God had lessons for me. This season had come by his choosing. What was I to learn; how was I to grow?

The patient acceptance of everything in its time is not something we find palatable. We like to take a more active role and change what we find unpleasant. To accept our current condition sounds too much like resignation. To this, wisdom says, "There's a time for change, and a time to accept things as given." Even exile is beautiful in its season.

We want to know how all of reality and life fit together, as well as what the right choice is at any given moment. Unfortunately, we cannot see time from beginning to end or know all the right options (moral absolutes the exception). But the wiser we become, the better we will fare—after all, wisdom informs us as to our seasons and our choices.

Walking the path of wisdom . . .

1. The author of *Ecclesiastes* wrote, "To everything there is a season; a time for every purpose under heaven" (3:1). Agree or disagree?
2. Does a patient acceptance of difficult circumstances sound too much like resignation to you or is there value to sometimes accepting things as given from above?
3. Does looking at a particular season of life as an opportunity to learn life's lesson make sense to you? Why or why not?

54.

Don't Think You Don't Belong

The lizard may be caught by the hands, yet it resides in the King's palaces (Proverbs 30:28).

One of our basic human needs is to be accepted. Unfortunately, it's common for people to feel like they don't belong, and they may feel this way because of rejection or abandonment. Whether within the family or social settings (e.g., work or school), typically people deal with feelings of not belonging by attempting to appease, rebel, or withdraw.

The excluded person may attempt to belong by appeasing those who reject him. He feels compelled to make up for any implied shortcomings. But it's impossible to appease the unappeasable, and his inevitable failure only strengthens his belief that he is unwanted or unloved. Convinced that others really are better and that he is a loser, he succumbs to this belief and accepts his "lowly" position in the system.

Other people might respond to exclusion by overtly rebelling or simply withdrawing, but in either case, they are saying the same thing: "If you don't want me, I don't need you." Truth be told, they long for love and acceptance, but it's too painful to acknowledge, so they deny, sometimes fiercely, any need. Their behavior typically alienates others, and so the experience of rejection is only compounded, which subsequently solidifies their belief that they don't need other people.

Instead of succumbing to these less-than-effective approaches to rejection, we can take a lesson from the *lizard*. The small house-lizard, also known as a gecko, has a peculiarity: It likes to live where people dwell. The gecko doesn't know that it doesn't belong. Whether condo or castle, the owner will attempt to remove the gecko from the property, but the gecko will return again and again.

The gecko instinctually knows that it belongs wherever it wishes, and we can have the same conviction. Instead of avoidance, we can repeatedly return to a situation or group and tell ourselves, "I belong." Instead of pacifying or rebelling, we can openly express our desire or need to be included. And if the exclusion continues, we can tell ourselves that the opinion of a few is of little consequence—we know who we are.

If we know our value, we won't have to feel hurt when others try to exclude us. We won't have to think that we don't belong. We can choose to act against this belief. Instead of avoiding, pacifying or rebelling, we can choose a healthier course of action. We can be like the gecko; he belongs wherever he wills.

Walking the path of wisdom . . .

1. Are there any situations or groups in which you feel excluded or unwanted? Why is that?
2. Do you ever take the approach of placating, rebelling, or withdrawing in those situations? What can you do to choose a healthier response?
3. What can you do to feel less like you don't belong? What actions can you take to make it more likely that you'll be welcomed?

55.

The Often Overlooked Dangers of Debt

The rich rule over the poor, and the borrower becomes the lender's slave (Proverbs 22:7).

When someone is in the position of a borrower, a servile outcome is the hidden danger of such indebtedness. The perpetual borrower loses his power to choose financial freedom.

The habit of revolving debt can become economically and emotionally debilitating. For instance, the more a person's debt increases, the fewer options he has if life becomes difficult or the economy tanks. What's more, the fewer his alternatives in financial hardship, the more he puts his emotional well being in jeopardy. Few things in life cause more anxiety or depression than financial uncertainty. A person in debt makes himself less than he could be financially and emotionally.

When we purchase with a credit card, it's similar to taking a double whammy. We are paying the price of the item—and whammy!—we are also paying interest on the price. Actually, we are cheating ourselves. We are paying more for items than they are worth, and the money going to interest is lost to any saving or investing. Ultimately, we make ourselves a *slave* to the credit card companies.

Work against extravagant spending and indebtedness. The theologian Matthew Henry once said, "Sell not your liberty to gratify your luxury." Accept that if you cannot pay cash for something, then you can't afford it. With effort and sacrifice, you can pay down debts and end the bondage to lenders.* You will also have money in hand to address present needs and supply future savings.

This is not to say that debt is never appropriate. In some cases, borrowing may be best. A series of adverse circumstances, which could not be foreseen or averted, may require the use of credit as a temporary solution. The use of someone else's money for leverage (e.g., a mortgage) may also be fitting. Use the wealth of lenders to advance yourself, not enslave yourself.

According to some researchers, wealthy people spend as if they earn half as much as they do, while debt-ridden consumers spend as if they earn twice as much as they do. Make yourself the former and not the latter. Instead of being under the thumb of a lender and enslaved to debt, achieve financial freedom by practicing the virtues of self-discipline and the merits of money management.

See also entries 36 and 74.

Walking the path of wisdom . . .

1. What are the hidden dangers of perpetual debt and credit card misuse?
2. Can you think of situations when debt might be appropriate? What can you do to protect yourself from the dangers of debt in those situations?
3. What steps can you take to deal with any current indebtedness and eliminate your debt?

NOTES:

* Several tools exist to help people eliminate their debts, including mortgages, in one half to one third the time simply by making better use of their existing money. Instead of serving the bank's interests, you can be your own bank. Learn more at: www.ThePathofWisdom.com/resources.htm.

56.

Integrity Works Just as Well as Bribery

Anyone who takes crooked paths will be found out, but the person of integrity walks securely. . . . [and] the person who hates bribes will live (Proverbs 10:9, 15:27).

Wisdom is frank in its appraisal of the pragmatic and readily admits that bribery can accomplish the ends desired (17:8), but our teacher is also clear that bribes threaten a man's soul and his home (15:27). The person who practices integrity and avoids bribes will protect himself and his home.

Bribery is any type of payment that serves to corrupt the behavior of another person. A gift becomes a bribe when the motive is to influence someone to do something in return, often something suspicious, indecent, or illegal. A bribe includes a sense of obligation, such as the bias of friendship or an unfair advantage, all of which entice.

Just about anyone can give into bribery, especially when it comes subtly, but the *person of integrity* resists bribery's allure. His integrity is more important than any object or any desire (Proverbs 16:8; 19:1; 28:6). He cannot be bought. Even if politicians, celebrities, or rock stars, who have sold their souls for influence or gain, parade before him, the person of integrity will refuse to fall in line. Most of the world says, "Show me the easy way," but the person of integrity declares, "Show me the right path."

A bribe usually accomplishes its purposes, but following integrity's track is likewise effective. A person conscious of her honest intent pursues her course with a clear conscience and no regret. She lives in blissful assurance. Integrity has its short term difficulties, yes, but it's much safer in the long run. Integrity's path leads to peace of mind and freedom from bribery's consequences.

Anyone who chooses integrity chooses wisely. Since integrity stays clear of all doubtful areas, it's the secure path. This path might appear to miss out on temporary advantages, but integrity's blessing lasts for time and eternity, beyond the material and immaterial. Whatever a person of integrity lacks according to the measure of this world is more than made up for in the abundance of what is not seen—joy, peace, and comfort.

Walking the path of wisdom . . .

1. When does something offered or given cross the line and become a bribe? Can you think of some examples of bribes?
2. What are the potential dangers of accepting a bribe, and what are the often overlooked advantages of living with integrity?
3. Why do people choose to accept bribes, and why do people find it difficult to choose the path of integrity? Is there anything that comes to mind that you could improve on when it comes to integrity?

57.

Love Covers a Multitude of Wrongs

Hatred stirs up dissension, but love covers over all wrongs (Proverbs 10:12, NIV).

We all wittingly and unwittingly commit wrongs against others. We may be the receiver or the perpetrator, but in either case, holding grievances or bearing *hatred* doesn't help anyone or solve anything. It simply *stirs up dissension* and widens rifts.

While writing this book, I had to face some personal offenses. During a time when I endured a great loss and traversed the wilderness of grief, I asked others to be there for me. Many came through with compassion and care, while others did little to comfort or understand (in either case, I accepted that no one could remove or replace my grief).

I thought: *How heartless of them* (the people who did little to comfort). But I recalled the many times that I chose to care for myself instead of consider the needs of someone else. Consequently, I chose to *cover* their *wrongs*. I decided to extend understanding and forgiveness.

When wrongs occur, love seeks to understand instead of condemn. We could ask ourselves (or the person directly): *Why would he (she) do that?* We can surmise (or receive) an answer that may help us extend understanding. For example, outbursts may be the protests of a hidden, but sad story in a person's past; meanness may be due to some poverty of spirit or resources; conceit may be someone's attempt to recover lost self-confidence; cruelty may simply be the familiar reaction of one deeply wounded; or rudeness may be due to some bravely borne illness unknown but to a chosen few. Love chooses to see what might be behind the offense.

When wrongs occur, love decides to forgive instead of hold a grudge. Forgiveness, the practice and process of not holding someone's offenses against them, softens the hearts of both parties. When forgiveness is given as generously as Jesus, a teacher of wisdom, suggested in the Gospels—seventy times seven—the practice may seem like weakness, but a person is never stronger than when he extends grace to another.

Covering refers to overlooking slights and offenses in the interest of peace and goodwill. Let us do what we wish others would do for us when we act wrongly. Let us in charity offer rays of understanding, forgiveness, and love, by seeing beyond any adverse behavior—forgetting much and forgiving much.

See also entry 66.

Walking the path of wisdom . . .

1. Why do people have a hard time letting go of wrongs committed against them? Do you struggle with the same problem? Why?
2. What do you think it means to love others when they wrong us?
3. How can covering the wrongs of others be a position of strength and not weakness?

58.

Don't Allow Yourself to Be Controlled by Excess

Listen my son, and be wise, and direct your heart in the right way. . . . for the heavy drinker and the glutton will meet with poverty (Proverbs 23:19, 21a).

The alcoholic or glutton is not the only one who allows his appetites to have dominion. A person could become controlled by or addicted to events, crises, possessions, behaviors, etc. When our hungers go unsatisfied or when our wounds go unhealed, we might turn to distractions or toxins to dull our pain. This gives our needs and wounds dominion over us, and the inevitable result is *poverty*—a literal loss or a perpetual emptiness.

In an attempt to identify any needs that control me, I have asked myself: *What needs am I trying to meet illegitimately?* I unearthed a few unhealthy approaches to people. I discovered that I occasionally attempt to control or manipulate people to act or think in a way that will appease me. I also found that I feel compelled to assert my rightness in discussions or disagreements. Similarly, I uncovered a need to be vindicated whenever I'm wronged or accused. What's more, I also found an insatiable longing to be accepted or to be the center of attention.

The charge to *direct your heart* refers to an ability to exercise control over wants and needs, and it applies to my unhealthy needs. This charge expects me to find an inside-out or healthy approach to my unhealthy needs.

Here's my inside out approach: First, instead of trying to control others or circumstances, I can seek to bring *calmness* to a situation. Second, when I need acceptance or attention, I'm operating out of emptiness, but I can choose to function as if I'm already *full.* Third, when I want vindication, I can place myself and the presumed injustice in *submission* to a higher authority, one who decides justly (for me, it's God). Last, instead of having to be right, I can choose to bring *shalom* (peace) into a discussion or dispute.

The person who *directs his heart* operates by self-governance and makes his needs and wounds his subjects. He rules over them; nothing destructive controls him. This person knows that he is not a victim of his impulses.* Instead of becoming a carbon copy of those seeking their personal ruin, he makes this life a joy and himself a tower of strength for others.

Walking the path of wisdom . . .

1. What is wrong with surrendering to our unhealthy or destructive tendencies? Why do we so rarely heed warnings against giving into these tendencies?
2. What needs or desires are you trying to meet in an illegitimate or unhealthy manner? What damage has this done to your life?
3. What might be a healthier approach to each of these needs or wants?

NOTES:

* Real change in the area of our needs or wants can be elusive, even for people with a serious commitment to self-improvement. Why? Well, unhealthy beliefs and thoughts govern our actions. *Affirming the Path* will assist you in creating the inner framework needed for living out the principles of *The Path of Wisdom*. Find it at: www.ThePathofWisdom.com/resources.htm.

59.

The Often Overlooked Hazards of Wealth

Whoever trusts in his riches will fall, but those who live rightly will thrive like a green branch (Proverbs 11:28).

We all want wealth, including those who rail against it. Some have called wealth an evil, but wealth is not evil in itself. It would be foolish, however, not to recognize that riches come with dangers. Perhaps the greatest test of character is not found in our lowest struggles but in our highest attainments. When we gain more, who do we become? Once we have wealth, wealth may smile and sneer, "Poor soul, he's not able to handle me."

The word *fall* in our proverb is an analogy meant to portray coming to ruin. Few acquire riches without acquiring other things: compromised values or rationalized offenses. The hazards of wealth are such that avarice and vanity are dressed in finery and mistaken as a higher good.

Take the example of a man who, after he has acquired wealth (or fame or success) in the city, returns to his hometown and tells everyone of his greatness. He says that he has returned to see the folks, but he has really returned so the folks can see him. He walks with a swagger and speaks with an arrogant tone. He is approaching the entrance of a dark valley—what William George Jordan called, "the dark valley of prosperity."

Jesus the great wisdom teacher said, "Much is required of those who have much" (Luke 12:48). If called upon to bear the great responsibility of wealth, let us bear it bravely and in simplicity, not allowing it to clutch us and force all that is decent from our person.

Those who are in wealth's grip may become dulled in conscience, but now and then wisdom will shine a ray of truth into their lives. If they can glimpse the ray, they will realize that somewhere along the way they lost trust, empathy, gentleness of nature, or other qualities they once held dear. "[The qualities] dropped away like a locket from an unguarded chain" (William George Jordan, *The Power of Purpose*, 58). Perhaps it's too late, but at that moment, they realize that wealth and prosperity are not life's greatest possessions.

The flourishing *green branch* represents well-being and prosperity. Those who seek to live rightly, honorably, and nobly, keeping money under the thumb of a higher purpose, are the truly wealthy. They live simply with faith in those who gird them, with love for those who are dear to them, and with a joy that fills them. Not surprisingly, they avoid the dark valley of wealth into which so many seem to stumble: They *thrive like a green branch*.

Walking the path of wisdom . . .

1. Has there been a time in your life when you noticed that material possessions didn't bring satisfaction?
2. How does one keep "money under the thumb of a higher purpose"?
3. What are some of the greater responsibilities of wealth?

60.

Be Wary of Wearing out Your Welcome

Seldom set foot in your neighbor's house, lest he become sick of you and despise you (Proverbs 25:17, NIV).

This proverb echoes a modern saying: "Familiarity breeds contempt." The sage warns that seeing too much of you could make your neighbor or friend despise you. When I was a kid, my mom called this wearing out your welcome. We are better off if we avoid becoming this kind of nuisance.

The expression *seldom set foot* is not suggesting that we avoid neighborly practice; it simply means that warm friendship cannot be maintained without consideration for everyone involved. One translation of this verse says, "Make your foot precious to your neighbor." Our feet become precious when we don't repeatedly put them across our neighbor's threshold.

Friendship is one of the sweet pleasures in life. There may be a temptation, however, to overindulge in a relationship. This behavior could inflict "nausea" on our friend or neighbor. Frequent visits without notice or constant pleas for companionship can wear out a neighbor's kindness and eventually cause displeasure or even disgust. Even if friends are closer than brothers, some level of consideration for a friend's time and needs is necessary.

I had two friends, Art and April, a welcoming and warm couple. Eventually, I unwittingly took advantage of their hospitality. I called too often or showed up too frequently. As a young newly married couple, they needed time to themselves, something I failed to consider in my own need for companionship. They sat me and a couple of other people down to let us know they needed more space and time for themselves.

One of the best ways to be well received by others is to give them the distance that we all need from time to time. Everyone needs space. Some need little; some need lots; but everyone needs it. Few people are frank enough to say, "Hey, I need some space." This means we need to be sensitive to when others might be growing tired of our presence. One way to tell how much time to spend with another (or at their place) is to note how much time the person spends with you (or at your place). The more or less the person is present will tell you the more or less "space" the person needs.

Wisdom is not only concerned with broad principles, but also includes specific courtesies. Good manners embody consideration for others. Let's be wary of perpetual or unreasonable intrusions upon a friend or neighbor. Let's accept that the quality of time spent together is more important than the quantity.

Walking the path of wisdom . . .

1. What things do people do to wear out their welcome? How often do you do these things with your friends or neighbors?
2. What problems could frequent or unannounced visits cause between friends or neighbors?
3. What steps can you take to respect your friend's or neighbor's space?

61.

Talking Too Much Will Make You a Nuisance

A chattering fool will be thrown down, but a person of good sense heeds instruction (Proverbs 10:8).

The *chattering fool* is the person who talks too much. The average person talks enough in a single day to fill a fifty-page book, but the chatterer could fill multiple volumes. The word *chattering* literally means "being much lipped." The chatterer's lips bring him ruin because everyone grows tired of listening to him.

At a social event or party, the chatterer is the one doing all the talking. This babbler speaks and monopolizes the conversation, and consequently, everyone thinks less of him. In a metaphorical sense, he is cast out or *thrown down*.

In about every seminary class I attended, at least one or two students would opine endlessly. Why did these "much lipped" people talk so much? Perhaps self-absorption ruled these babblers. In other words, they liked the sound of their own voice. Perhaps they were uncomfortable with silence. But there's nothing wrong with silence. Whether it was self-absorption, fear of silence, or something else, they made a nuisance of themselves by talking endlessly.

Most of us would prefer not to irritate others with our words. One solution is to go on a word diet. A diet is typically understood as cutting down on how much one eats, but you can also do the same with words—cutting down on the number of words you use. When you say less, you focus on the quality of your words. Here are some suggestions for going on a word diet:

1. Purposely decide not to talk. When you feel compelled to speak, opt instead to keep silent. Ask yourself, "Does this really need to be said?"

2. Use nonverbal communication. Instead of talking, try nodding, smiling, frowning, or raising a single eyebrow (if you can do that).
3. Try to under talk. Become a man or woman of few words. Use restraint with your words; understate rather than overexplain. Say as little as possible.

Instead of being the person everyone dismisses, the chatterer could become the person everyone heeds. All he has to do is use fewer words. For instance, a college buddy of mine did not say much. He weighed his words carefully before he spoke. When he did speak, people seemed to respect whatever he said. And what about us? We could be a much lipped person, such as the chattering fool, or we could be like my friend—*a person of good sense*. Who would you rather be: the babbling fool or someone worth hearing?

Walking the path of wisdom . . .

1. Do you know someone who talks too much? Does he or she ever get on your nerves?
2. How about you? Do think people see you as a chattering fool or someone worth hearing?
3. Do you think the suggestions for going on a word diet might help you to become more respected in the use of your words? Why or why not?

62.

Make Your Marriage Perpetually Vibrant

Anyone who finds a spouse finds a good thing and has received God's favor (Proverbs 18:22).

Your spouse is a gift from above, even if at times it seems like the marriage originates from below. Few things come naturally, and marriage is no exception. Solomon offers some suggestions for making a marriage happy, fulfilling, and more like the *favor* God intended.

Cultivate friendship in your marriage (Proverbs 27:8–9). The physical aspect of love is not enough to make a marriage last—that requires friendship. Research shows that passionate love in a marriage has a life span of about two years, and if a husband and wife are not good friends by this time, the marriage will die. The likelihood of a marriage lasting "till death" increases significantly when spouses are not only lovers but also friends.

Avoid gossiping about your spouse (Proverbs 17:9). An icicle melts one drip at a time. A single drip is not the end of the icicle, but all the drips together destroy the whole. Similarly, gossiping about your spouse brings an end to the marriage one drip at a time. When shortcomings and problems arise with your spouse or marriage and talking to your spouse doesn't seem to help, friends and relatives are rarely good options for counsel. Instead, turn to a therapist, minister, or health-care professional. They offer privacy, impartiality, and confidentiality.

Treat your spouse courteously (Proverbs 15:23). How strange it is when a spouse treats strangers with more respect than the husband or wife. He opens doors for others, but not for his wife. She says please and thank you, except to her husband. Such courtesies should start at home then overflow to others. Men, when was the last time you opened the car door for your wife? Women, when was the last time you thanked your husband? "A word fitly spoken [or an action timely done] is like apples of gold in settings of silver" (Proverbs 25:11).

Work at your marriage (Proverbs 14:1). Anything worth having is worth the effort, and to take your relationship to a deeper level will require work. Make time for you and your spouse to be alone together. Use this time to deepen your relationship. Explore intimacy in ways other than the physical (e.g., intellectual intimacy, emotional affection).

Someone has said that a successful marriage requires falling in love many times over but with the same person. Marriages encounter numerous difficulties: illness, poor finances, or unemployment, to name a few, but with some effort you can make your relationship perpetually vibrant—and an instrument of *favor*.

Walking the path of wisdom . . .

1. Does your relationship with your wife or husband seem like a divine favor or something else entirely?
2. If you're having problems in your marriage, can you see the value in talking with a trained professional instead of friends or family?
3. Anything worth having is worth the work and this includes marriage. What can you do this week to be more courteous toward your spouse? What could you do to cultivate friendship and greater intimacy?

63.

What Is Wrong with Everyone Else?

Good sense enables a person to defer any frustration, and glory comes to him who overlooks an offense (Proverbs 19:11).

I once had a friend who was fond of saying, "Life would be great if it weren't for the people." Perhaps you can relate. The problems in our lives often seem to be due to others (or so we think).

You get on the highway, and then suddenly notice the red light flashing on the dashboard. The gas tank is on empty. *Just great! Not a gas station for miles.* Immediately, your thoughts go to who last drove the vehicle—your spouse, teenager, or neighbor:

Why didn't he fill up the tank?

She knew I needed the car today.

Why does he always do this to me?

How often do we look for someone to blame when something goes wrong? The reason for the blame is often due to the injection of *should* or *should not* into the context. We attach to an event a belief about what someone else *should* or *should not* have done. Consequently, something that "just is" becomes something frustrating.

In the case of the empty gas tank, blaming a husband, wife, teenager, or whoever last drove the car, doesn't fix the situation. Instead, you compound the problem. Now, not only are you anxious about running out of gas, but you are also angry. You think that your spouse, friend, or teenager does not care enough (or is too thoughtless) to make sure the gas tank is full. But that's just an assumed belief to give the situation meaning—and a not too helpful meaning at that. The truth of the matter could simply be that the person didn't notice the tank was nearly empty.

Most frustrating events are neutral. It's you and I who imbue them with meaning. So why not give the situation a more neutral or even positive connotation (an exercise in *good sense*)? Instead of assuming someone doesn't care, you could think: *He didn't realize that the tank was on empty*. This will be freeing to you and to the person you're blaming.

The Hebrew word for *glory* is sometimes translated *beauty* and, in the proverb, alludes to the adornment we wear when we overlook an offense. Even God himself discloses his power chiefly through his mercy. When our thoughts turn to accusations, let's give whomever we're blaming the benefit of the doubt by simply answering our assumptions with something more neutral.

Walking the path of wisdom . . .

1. Do you ever think: *Life would be great if it weren't for the people*? But are other people really the problem?
2. It seems common for people to look for someone to blame when things go wrong? Why do we do that?
3. Is there someone or several people whom you tend to blame when things go wrong? What measures can you take so you don't assume another person is to blame?

64.

Your Tongue Has the Power to Destroy or Inspire

Death and life are in the power of the tongue, and those who cherish it will eat its fruit (Proverbs 18:21).

The best words to speak are not usually the first words that come to mind, especially if the words are inspired by anger, frustration, or resentment. If we utter harsh words, then the tongue destroys or even kills. Not a literal death, of course, but cruel words can kill a person's spirit. This is the *fruit* of a tongue that speaks rashly; it brings about *death*.

Whatever we say should be for the purpose of building up others, not to tear them down. If we use positive, encouraging language, then our tongue gives life to a person's spirit. This is the *fruit* of the tongue that edifies; it gives *life*.

A Japanese proverb says, "One kind word can warm for three months of winter." In a cold and harsh world, we desperately need warming words. How can we exchange destructive language for uplifting words?

The solution is to guard our speech. The word *guard* is a military term meaning to stand watch. A soldier on guard is alert, watching for enemy forces that may attempt to infiltrate. Let's apply the concept to our speech.

First, we guard the *content* of what we say (Proverbs 21:23). Guarding content means we are vigilant, consciously checking words and verbal patterns. The wise person puts his mind in gear before he puts his mouth in motion. He runs the words through his mind and weighs their potential effect.

Second, we guard the *manner* of what we say (Proverbs 15:28). Manner refers to tone, and our tone should be gracious and kind. Tone communicates as much as the words themselves. The person of wisdom thoughtfully considers her tone and makes sure that it's not hurtful or disrespectful.

Third, we guard the *timing* of what we say (Proverbs 5:23). A proper word spoken at the wrong time can be just as damaging as a thoughtless comment. It could be that a person is not ready to accept what we have to say. Perhaps she is angry; perhaps he is wounded. In either case, what we say won't be well received. The possessor of wisdom makes sure his words are needful for the moment.

Saying the right thing in the right way at the right time is not a simple skill. But if we guard our speech and practice using our tongue beneficially, in time our words will bear good fruit—fruit that gives life.

See also entry 42.

Walking the path of wisdom . . .

1. Have you said anything recently that you wish you could take back? What are the most life-giving words you've spoken lately?
2. How can you ensure that you use your tongue to inspire?
3. Whom can you think of that you need to inspire? What will you say to this person? When will you say it?

65.

Determine the Legitimacy of Shame

When wrongdoing comes, contempt also comes, and with the onset of shame comes loathing (Proverbs 18:3).

Shame is a complex subject. On one hand, shame can come as a consequence of some wrongdoing, and thus may be legitimate. On the other hand, much of the shame and loathing we feel is not due to some wrongdoing, but due to a perceived deficiency in our dignity. So in this case, the shame is illegitimate.

According to the Hebrew tradition, each person possesses dignity as an image bearer of God, but individuals can easily lose sight of their dignity. If we perceive personal attacks from our past as attacks on our dignity, then we might feel as though we have less dignity. We come to feel exposed. That is, we begin to feel ashamed.

Eventually, we come to hate the exposed parts of our person. If our weight is exposed, we will hate our bodies; if our nose is exposed, we will hate our face; if our desire to be loved is exposed, we will hate the longing to be loved. When we loathe ourselves and see parts of ourselves as despicable, although they are intrinsic to our dignity, we let illegitimate shame take over our feelings.

For example, I have had more than my fair share of failure with women (many men can relate). When a woman would reject me, I would feel foolish for even being interested in her. I eventually came to feel and believe it was wrong to express an interest in a woman. I felt exposed anytime someone knew I was interested. I felt shameful over something that was completely natural, something intrinsic to my dignity as a man.

When we repeatedly ascribe failure or shortcoming to our legitimate longings, as I did with my failure with women, we may eventually feel ashamed and loathe ourselves for being so foolish as to hope or desire. But this hope or longing is intrinsic to our dignity and completely legitimate. There's nothing wrong with us that we should feel ashamed about ourselves. We have been unable to meet our longing, which means, we have experienced a loss. And in the case of a loss, a healthier response would be to feel disappointment or sadness. Feelings like disappointment make more sense than the extreme of hating ourselves.

Certain parts of our person, including certain longings, reflect our intrinsic dignity, and when a longing goes unfulfilled, we may hate the part of us that longs or sees ourselves as being at fault. But no moral wrong has been done, so there is no reason for shame. Let's be gentle with ourselves and choose rightful disappointment over illegitimate shame.

Walking the path of wisdom . . .

1. Do you accept that you have an intrinsic dignity as a person? Why or why not?
2. Are there parts of yourself that you feel badly about, ashamed about, even though they are a good and important part of your person and dignity? How did you come to feel this illegitimate shame?
3. Do you think sadness or disappointment might be more fitting in the case of illegitimate shame?

66.

There's Nothing Wrong With Taking Time to Rest

The fear of the Lord leads to life, so that one may rest—satisfied and safe from evil (Proverbs 19:23).

Anyone who fears the Lord reaps many rewards. Chief among them is real and lasting life, but according to this proverb, rest is also a significant benefit. Wisdom's way suggests that a healthy respect for God includes diligent pursuits, work that leads to true life and lasting security. And anyone who has worked deserves to rest. Satisfying rest is one of the many fruits of labor.

The charge in the Hebrew tradition to keep the Sabbath refers to the cessation of ordinary work for one day out of seven. This day is set aside as a time to worship God, but equally significant is humanity's inherent need for rest. Leisure, play, and rest all have a proper and fitting place; they are worthwhile practices. Actually, rest is commanded. One would think the command to rest to be one command we would not resist—but we do.

When it comes to rest and work, the Western mind takes a distorted position. We seem to think that our time off or our play must be practical or contribute to our work. This pragmatic approach to rest, however, makes for a miserable life. Utilitarian rest cannot provide the much-needed break from the demands of work and life.

In a similar distorted view, we think of leisure in terms of convenience and luxury. In order to rest, we think we must go somewhere and spend a lot. This means many of us can't afford leisure. The needed rest just gets put off. And if we do go on vacation, we do not truly relax. We are in such a hurry that we're unable to have fun, or we're too worried about meeting the trip's grand expectations to enjoy the experience.

For our purposes, the word rest does not mean idleness; it means relaxing, playing, and worshiping. The word refers to a "doing" that has no other purpose than unwinding or celebrating. Accordingly, your rest does not have to be inactive, but ideally it will avoid the pragmatic approach typical of western rest.

How can we attain this intentional rest? We need to let go of any less-than-healthy attitudes toward rest and work. Also, we need to find ways to refresh that are not pragmatic. Let's make relaxing and enjoying life the only purpose of our rest and refreshment. Taking time to rest and enjoy the fruits of our labor will make our lives more satisfying.

Walking the path of wisdom . . .

1. Why do so many have such a hard time following the command to rest?
2. Do you agree or disagree with the assertion that we in the West have a twisted view of rest? Where do we go wrong in our understanding and use of rest?
3. What can you do to improve the nature and quality of rest for you and your family?

67.

Greed Is Counter Productive

A person with an eye toward greed hurries after riches, but he does not know that poverty awaits him (Proverbs 28:22).

The person who gives into greed may act contrary to his higher self in order to satisfy the insatiable need for more. He may break laws, cut corners, cheat customers, bribe legislators, and in the process of pursuing *riches*, he may come upon literal or metaphorical *poverty*.

For example, an author of a best-selling book might have taken great care in making his message right, but he may befall the vertigo of the money that follows and, with his next book, hastily rush it into print. But the new book will more than likely fail, because the author didn't give it the necessary care that brought the success of the first.

An artist may not repeat her initial success if she takes shortcuts in her subsequent work. This later work might superficially represent her style but will probably lack the depth and complexity of the originals. Not surprisingly then, her new work does not receive the same acclaim or produce the same monetary return, yet she wonders why.

The businessman who starts small and eventually reaps a cornucopia of rewards may find it hard to "keep his feet on the ground." If he abandons the very practices that brought him success, looking for quicker, cheaper means to more, then these new, shoddy practices will probably result in losses.

Greed refers to the pursuit or trust in money as the power able to affect a better life. Greed's destructive qualities apply not only to someone who has gained and wants more, but also to people with little who think that acquiring more will finally make them happy. Sadly, though, when they get what they think will give them happiness, usually the happiness is missing, and the consequence is greater despondency or deepening poverty.

Greed makes one who started out with noble pursuits and high ideals into a different person, unrecognizable perhaps. To accumulate more, the greedy invariably compromise who they are. Their insatiable quest for more eventually kills their higher affections.

The problem with greed is that it equates acquiring money and possessions with true living; it becomes a substitute for the truly enriching and rewarding pursuits of life. As Jesus the great wisdom teacher said, "A person's life does not consist in the abundance of his possessions" (Luke 12:15). The greedy pursuit of riches has a way of aiming at what ultimately doesn't matter. True life, real living, does not depend on what one possesses.

Walking the path of wisdom . . .

1. What is the problem with greed? Why is it that those who are greedy are rarely satisfied?
2. Can you identify any greed within your circle of friends or within yourself? Can you identify other pursuits of life that might have greater value than the pursuit of riches?
3. How can you keep from becoming greedy?

68.

Practice the True Nature of Love

Do not let love and faithfulness depart from you. Bind them around your neck; write them upon your heart (Proverbs 3:3).

In a beloved Hebrew story, Elimelech leads his family out of famine-ridden Israel into Moab in search of a better life, but unfortunately the patriarch dies upon arrival. Not long after his death, his widow, Naomi, suffers another loss: Her two sons die, leaving their mother and widowing their wives. Convinced that God has dealt bitterly with her, Naomi decides to return to Israel. The stage is set for the unfolding events known as the story of *Ruth*.

The main characters in the *Ruth* narrative practice an approach to people and life called *hesed*. The term has confounded Hebrew scholars for centuries, but the meaning is similar to that of "love demonstrated in loyalty." *Hesed* is a kind of love, a true love that persists. Romantic love might bring a couple to the wedding altar, but only *hesed* sustains a marriage and persists through the inevitable changes in life.

This true love involves an unusual level of commitment to another. One daughter-in-law, Ruth, the namesake of the story, does the unexpected. Instead of staying among her people and remarrying a Moabite man, she insists on going with Naomi to Israel. In contrast, the other daughter-in-law did the ordinary and returned to her family, which was not wrong, but it was not *hesed*. Once in Bethlehem, as a further demonstration of *hesed*, instead of seeking a marriage to benefit herself, Ruth sought a marriage that would assist her mother-in-law, a union to a kinsman redeemer. (This redeemer is relative who can restore "wholeness" to Elimelech's property and family—notably Naomi.)

This true love entails an extraordinary willingness to risk for another. During one night, Ruth takes the risk of lying on the threshing floor at the feet of the only remaining kinsman redeemer. In that culture, this behavior was tantamount to a marriage proposal. A woman proposing to a man? How would Boaz, the potential redeemer, respond to a woman's forwardness—anger, embarrassment, acceptance? And although her actions were innocent, if she had been discovered, she could have ruined Boaz's reputation, not to mention her own. Nevertheless, Ruth carried out this perilous behavior in the hope of securing Naomi's survival.

Let your love be like that of Ruth's. All during my childhood, my mom repeatedly modeled this type of love, sacrificing for her children—going without so we would have what we needed. I only wish I came close to her example, the same example set by Ruth. Practice the true nature of love: devotion, commitment, and risk. Write this love on your heart, and do not let it *depart from you*.

Walking the path of wisdom . . .

1. How difficult do you find it to practice the type of love described above?
2. How often does devotion and commitment come into play in the practice of love?
3. How often does risk for another come into play in your practice of love?

69.

Drunken Fun Is Not Worth the Potential Damage

Wine is a mocker, strong drink a brawler, and whoever is deceived by either is not wise (Proverbs 20:1).

The love of alcohol typically proves to be a vice more dangerous than it initially seems. Solomon described alcohol as a *mocker* and a *brawler*, and these qualities apply to anyone who misuses alcohol. *Wine is a mocker*. It depresses our inhibitions, and we make fools of ourselves. *Strong drink is a brawler*. It lowers our self-control, and our tempers flare. Alcohol's sway is so powerful that the foolish victim repeatedly consents to being deceived by its lure.

Many use alcohol to create an unreal world they can live in for a time. If you're unhappy in reality, when drunk, you feel happy. If you're inhibited in reality, when drunk, you seem to be free. If you feel inferior most days, when drunk, you seem stronger. But these altered states are only for a time being.

Drunkenness might provide brief relief or merriment, but it's foolish to find respite or joy in something that also causes such an accumulation of woes. To place one's pleasure in the hands of a cruel companion such as alcohol, *is not wise*—it's just plain foolish. Anyone given to excessive drinking is not accused of sin against God; his offense is against himself. His conduct is self-destructive and incompatible with the path of wisdom, which seeks the well-being of the individual.

There are several steps we can take to avoid alcohol's sway. Step one: Decide that you're going to discipline yourself. Discipline is a conscious effort to submit your will to your higher values. This includes a refusal to surrender yourself to potentially destructive influences. Step two: Consciously and deliberately exercise your will and conquer your tendency to give into alcohol. Resist the urge;

refuse it. And remember, any exception you tolerate makes it easier to surrender to the next exception. Step three: If you're given to drunkenness, accept that alcohol is a soil in which no life grows. Your best bet is to find positive substitutes for alcohol misuse.

When we see drunks acting like fools, or if we fall into that trap ourselves, let's remind ourselves of the feelings of foolishness and emptiness that follow, not to mention the throbbing headache. Let's ensure that we're not *deceived* by alcohol's allure; instead, let's exercise self-discipline. And if we have trouble stopping, then let's allow others to set the limits and hold us to them. Better yet, if we have a tendency to get drunk, we may want to pass up that first drink altogether.

Walking the path of wisdom . . .

1. What is your attitude toward the use of alcohol?
2. What is wrong with drunkenness? What damages does it cause? Why are warnings against drunkenness so rarely heeded?
3. How can you overcome tendencies to drink too much?

70.

End Sexual Impropriety Before It Ends You

The person who commits sexual impropriety lacks sense; whoever does so destroys his soul (Proverbs 6:32).

Wisdom celebrates the beauty of sexual fidelity but makes it clear that sexual indiscretion only leads to a self-inflicted destruction. Obviously, this is contrary to the supposed wisdom of today that urges people, especially young people, to find satisfaction and pleasure in sexual impropriety. But this sexual recklessness demonstrates a complete lack of *sense*—it offers nothing but pain and loss.

Sexual indiscretion destroys people emotionally (Proverbs 6:27–28). According to the Hebrew tradition, a sexual relationship with someone gives physical expression to what it means to be bound to another person emotionally and spiritually. To give yourself to another physically and then withhold yourself emotionally and spiritually engages you in a destructive lie, a split in your person that can only lead to emotional and spiritual pain.

Sexual indiscretion does not build a house. In *Proverbs*, the image of a house symbolizes security and shelter. Promiscuity, by contrast, scatters one's resources. One of the quickest and surest ways to ruin a home is through sexual indiscretion. What a person possesses in fidelity, a person loses in infidelity: loyalty, love, intimacy, and family. Building a home takes a long time, which requires patience and sacrifice. The pseudo intimacy of sexual indiscretion may come more easily, but it only satisfies for the moment.

Sexual indiscretion causes injury and fury (Proverbs 6:30–31). A petty thief may get a light punishment, but that's not the case if someone engages in sexual impropriety. This person is sentenced to lasting wounds. A man's (or woman's) power should be invested in his family, but instead, someone not bound to him diminishes and exploits his emotions and resources. Furthermore, those wronged by the man's impropriety may retaliate in jealousy and rage; he faces needless and unending battles. But one of the biggest wounds is this: he brings lasting disgrace to his name.

Wisdom's instruction: Close off seduction to every avenue of your senses. Close your mind to anything acquainted with sexual impropriety; close your heart to any desire for indiscretion. Furthermore, keep clear of tempting situations, which in practical terms may mean that you change your job or break with a group of friends. Moreover, turn to divine strength for help. God's intervention may save you from personal destruction or worse.

Walking the path of wisdom . . .

1. What would cause a person to engage in sexual indiscretion, even if his moral beliefs tell him it's wrong?
2. What do you make of the consequences given above for sexual indiscretion? Agree or disagree?
3. What are some ways you can avoid sexual temptation?

71.

Take a Stand for What Is Just and Right

Open your mouth for those who cannot speak for themselves, not to mention, those who cannot help themselves. Speak up and judge fairly; plead the cause of the poor and needy (Proverbs 31:8–9).

This proverb is written as instruction for a king and charges the king to act as royalty should—powerfully on behalf of those *who cannot help themselves.* Our own royal status (you didn't know you're royalty?) should compel us to act similarly.

The story of Esther, a dearly loved Hebrew account of love, hate, and intrigue, set in the splendor of the Persian Empire, tells of a young woman. This woman rose from her lowly, orphaned status to the highest position possible: Queen of Persia.

After Xerxes, the King of the Empire, banished his first queen for defiance, he sought a new queen from a vast array of hand-selected virgins. From this diverse group, he chose his new wife—a young Hebrew woman, Esther, the namesake of the story.

The Hebrews, a subjugated people, were not permitted to usurp their position. But one Hebrew leader, named Mordechai, did just that: He refused to bow to a Persian emissary. The offended Persian suggested to the king that the Hebrews were a problem people and should be destroyed. Xerxes agreed, not knowing that his new queen was a Hebrew.

Mordechai convinced Esther that she must approach the king to save her people, but since Xerxes was ever mindful of assassination, to come into his presence without permission would mean certain death, even for the new queen. But come she did. She identified herself as a Hebrew and pleaded with the king to spare her people. Xerxes decided to issue an edict allowing the Hebrews to defend themselves. Because of Esther's efforts, the Hebrews not only defended themselves, they did more—they soundly defeated the forces of the offended official. Esther did what one would expect of royalty.

In Hebrew wisdom literature, humans are ascribed a position a little lower than the angels, which means all humans are intrinsically royal. From an early age, we need to learn that we are royalty and how to live in accordance with that status—to help the helpless and speak for the powerless.

Your story is not the same as Esther's situation, but you still encounter injustice and wrongs. Wisdom expects a response. You may rail or act against the offenses you experience, as the proverb suggests, but standing against injustice also entails personal responsibility. Wisdom says to us, "Here is an example of justice; now measure yourself accordingly."

In a world where injustice is the typical principle of operation, let us speak and act on behalf of the wronged or needy. But also let us live justly. Anyone who walks the way of wisdom also walks the path of justice and acts like royalty.

See also entry 13.

Walking the path of wisdom . . .

1. Why is justice so important? To whom does it apply?
2. How can you cultivate justice in your areas of influence?
3. Is there someone within your realm of influence that needs someone to speak up for him or her (perhaps a child, a person with disabilities, or an elderly person)?

72.

Don't Expect to Prosper Without Action

One who is slack in his work is akin to one who wastes away. . . . but the work of a person's hands will return to him (Proverb 18:9, 12:14).

We reap what we sow. This saying is known as the law of recompense. There's a fundamental principle implicit in this law: One cannot expect to reap without sowing. In other words, only the person who puts his hands to work will get a return.

For whatever reason, people tend to approach the law of recompense from a negative perspective, that whenever you do something wrong, you can be sure to face the consequences. There is truth to this, but there's also a positive take: "He who sows what is right gets a true reward" (Proverbs 11:18). If we "sow" (take a proper course of action), then it's possible that we will reap a "true reward" (prosper in some manner).

This positive outcome is only possible in one scenario: we must sow. We can't expect a *return* without doing *the work*. My mom enjoys gardening, and I recall as a kid looking in the kitchen drawer and finding packages of seeds. The seeds weren't going to grow sitting in the drawer; someone had to plant them (which my mom gladly did).

Like seeds left in a drawer, perhaps we wait to do what is right or to pursue some ambition. Maybe we have good reason for waiting, or maybe we're just being complacent, but in either case the result is the same: We become like *one who wastes away*. In other words, we bring disorder or ruin to our lives. This wasting away can be imperceptible and perhaps as pleasant as falling sleep.

If a person will choose to be diligent, regardless of the obstacles, then she will add to her life inspiration and strength.* She will become a person who does her best at all times, and that determination will bear fruit in every part of her life. Not surprisingly, her work will return to her.

Typically, most people would rather do as little as possible while thinking or expecting to get the best in return. Conversely, wisdom's way is to put our utmost talent and skill to work so life can *return* its best to us. But a cautionary note: While there is truth in the law of recompense, we can't expect or require a certain outcome. The law of recompense is a general principle, not an absolute. Even so, let's give this law its best opportunity to come through. Let's put our hands to work.

See also entries 34 and 94.

Walking the path of wisdom . . .

1. Do you recognize any procrastination in yourself? Do you think it is a serious problem?
2. Can you think of an area in which you need to be more diligent?
3. Is there something you've given up on, perhaps a dream or an ambition that you could pick up and pursue again? What kinds of things tend to stop you from moving forward with your talent and skill?

NOTES:

* Sustaining real or transformative change is difficult. A key reason, other than procrastination, is that unhealthy beliefs govern our actions. *Affirming the Path* will assist you in creating the right inner "framing" for living out wisdom's principles. Visit www.ThePathofWisdom.com/resources.htm.

73.

Companionship Is Preferred to Isolation

Like a bird that strays from her nest, so is a person who wanders from his place. Perfume and incense make the heart glad, and a friend's company is pleasant to the soul. Do not drift from your friends (Proverbs 27:8–10).

A bird knows by instinct that the nest is a place of safety. When a bird wanders, it can wind up isolated and in danger. It's no less senseless for a person to drift from family or friends. What is life without the enriching blessing of companionship?

In any city and on every countryside, thousands of people live alone. The experience of loneliness can range from a vague restlessness to a painful emptiness. But for sure, lonely people share a longing. They want someone with whom they can share the inconsequential things of life—not to mention their joys and sorrows.

Loneliness is not limited to people living alone; it can also persist among families. Some families appear to have companionship but lack true closeness and intimacy. Two or more people can live in the same house but be emotionally distant. They create their own loneliness.

For some people, including me, emotional distancing comes easier than being in relationships. Work, family, and society have their claim on us, and we might need to escape at times. But this occasional need for space is different than the habitual practice of isolation and distancing.

Typically, we distance ourselves because of past or present familial relationships. We avoid people and situations that feel similar to the intensity or pain experienced in our families. When we have been hurt by family members, especially repeatedly, we become seized by a desire not to be hurt by anyone again. This powerful and controlling feeling pushes us away from others.

The solution to distancing or drifting is to make the effort to re-engage people. Simple, yes, but not easily done. Here is the twist: When we do re-engage, we must do so with the intent to give. This can be as simple as putting a smile on someone's face. Ironically, when we help others forget their longings and sorrows, we silence the rumblings of our own soul.

Just as oil and perfume refresh the senses, a friend's or relative's companionship can be pleasant and refreshing to the soul. The harsh realities of sorrow and trouble seem to soften with companionship. Let's seek out relationships with others—*and make the heart glad.*

Walking the path of wisdom . . .

1. Do you find friendship or companionship refreshing to the soul? Why or why not?
2. Are there family members or friends with whom you haven't kept in touch with lately?
3. With whom do you need to re-engage, and how will you do that? What could you do to change the distancing?

74.

Seek Release From Foolish Indebtedness

If you have foolishly put up surety, whether for your neighbor or stranger, then my son, to seek release, do this . . . Go, humble yourself, and persistently plead with the other person. Deliver yourself, like a gazelle fleeing a hunter's hand or a bird taking flight from a fowler's snare (Proverbs 6:1, 3, 5).

This proverb comes in the context of seeking release from surety (securing another person's debt). But it also applies more generally to any foolish indebtedness, which arises out of one or more scenarios: borrowing more than can be reasonably paid back, attempting to buy items without the ability to pay cash, and using credit for means other than leverage.

Consider this: Every time you take on a creditor, put a new credit card in your wallet, or buy a car with a loan, you have taken on a business partner. In an equal partnership, revenue is divided equally among the partners. That is not the case when it comes to credit. Instead, you become the junior partner, and your revenue goes to the senior partners—the creditors.

Credit card companies bank on you charging more and more purchases and falling prey to increasing interest payments. If you're not careful, you can be manipulated into debt or poverty. Have you been trapped or ensnared? Perhaps, but you likewise share responsibility for poor choices and foolishly allowing yourself to fall into their hands.

It doesn't make sense to owe your life to a creditor. *Deliver yourself.* Ideally, you do this by paying off the debt. However, if this is increasingly difficult or no longer possible, consider release through negotiation. Call the credit company and negotiate a cut in your interest rate or monthly payment. If the person you talk to won't help you, ask for a supervisor, and if that doesn't work, make repeated calls.

If you're financial position prevents you from paying a creditor or collector, seek a settlement. Put together a financial statement showing that your liabilities exceed your assets. You may need an accountant's assistance. Send the statement with a letter to the creditor explaining that you do not have the ability to pay. You will probably have to persist to obtain a settlement. If your efforts go unattended, or if you feel this is an overwhelming task, you can turn to a debt negotiation service—people who will *plead* on your behalf.

Buying on credit can make you a slave to creditors. The habitual borrower loses the ability to keep money in his wallet. Whatever he makes goes to another, but he (and you) can change the situation by seeking release—*like a gazelle fleeing a hunter.*

See also entries 36 and 55.

Walking the path of wisdom . . .

1. If you are in debt, how do you feel about being in debt? Do you feel content, or do you feel ensnared?
2. If you are in debt, how did you get there? What can you do to prevent debt in the future?
3. What are some steps you can take to reduce your current debt?

75.

Be at Peace With Yourself

Better is he who is despised and has only one servant, than he who admires himself but lacks bread (Proverbs 12:9).

Anyone who attempts to be esteemed or recognized by others, but in the process deprives himself of what is truly necessary (such as bread), makes himself a slave to others' opinions. The deprivation could be anything important, such as relationships or morals. You see, some people will sacrifice the most elemental aspects of themselves in order to have the approval of others.

I don't know about you, but for much of my life, I have given too much importance to what other people think. This unhealthy need for acceptance or approval has led me to compromise my beliefs or values (the elemental).

In the Hebrew context, a person who had *one servant* did not possess enough to gain the esteem of the wealthy. He was despised. Similarly, perhaps you feel despised. Perhaps you feel that others don't consider you worthwhile. Regardless of what others think, make a habit of esteeming yourself. Fight destructive thoughts and stubbornly refuse to allow distorted self-abuse. Ultimately, your thoughts, and not someone's opinions, determine how you will view yourself. Make a habit of approving yourself.

Affirm yourself with this exercise: Stand in front of the mirror, look yourself in the eye, and speak out loud. Say the opposite of the negative stuff you usually believe about yourself. Verbally endorse yourself, whether for big or small things, even things in the past. Now, you're probably thinking: *You can't be serious. I'm supposed to stand in front of the mirror and talk to myself.* Yes—do it. The result will be a vast difference in your self-perception.

If someone does not approve of us, it probably has more to do with his problems, preferences, or irrational beliefs than with us. From now on, let no one trouble us. If someone wants to reject us, treat us rudely or unkindly, that's his problem. Those who show their disapproval probably lack the grace that comes with an awareness of their own faults. This deficiency obliges our compassion (for them) and not our flagellation (of self).

It's the ruin of the self-deceived to view themselves more highly than they ought. Similarly, it's the shortcoming of the upright to think less of ourselves than we should. We must cease the endless thoughts or beliefs that invalidate ourselves. We possess the power to be at peace with ourselves. *Shalom*, be at peace, especially with ourselves.

See also entry 54.

Walking the path of wisdom . . .

1. What do you make of the saying, "We are often more gracious to others than we are to ourselves"? What negative things do you constantly tell yourself?
2. Does your view of yourself or others match reality? Do you overly esteem other people to the detriment of your own self-perception?
3. What do you think about the exercise to affirm yourself in the mirror?

76.

Make an Account of Your Blessings

Remove vanity and foolish thoughts far from me. Give me neither poverty nor riches, but give me only the necessities of life (Proverbs 30:8).

We live with so much dissatisfaction. The sage Agur, the author of this proverb, had apparently fallen into dissatisfaction. He needed to set right his foolish thoughts. Similarly, rightful thoughts can help us realize that what we have is sufficient. We call this perspective *contentment*. One of the best ways to develop contentment is to take into account our many blessings.

When foolish thoughts run free, we tend to view our situation as comparatively unfortunate. We come to believe that life hands us a basketful of sorrows and gives our neighbor the occasional trouble wrapped in a box of truffles. What we see in our neighbors, though, does not represent the whole of their sorrow; nor does what we notice in ourselves represent the sum of our circumstances. We forget that we only see part of their trials, and we forget to count much of our good.

We typically exaggerate our misery because we measure our lives by what we lack. While it's fitting to occasionally assess our lives, we tend to look at life all wrong—with a focus on the debits. Life is like a ledger with debits on one side and credits on the other. The good in life is not seen in the debit column nor the credit column, but at the bottom where the net or the equity is calculated. We forget the equity.

What seems to us a gross injustice is probably just a focus on our debits. We see our sorrows through the magnifying glass of discouragement, making them greater than mountains. We see our joys through the reducing glass of unmet expectations, diminishing them to nothingness. We become so heavy with what we have to bear that we ignore any reason for levity. We count our problems and not our blessings. We fail to see the balance of blessings still available to us (at the bottom of the ledger).

Give me neither poverty nor riches is another way of saying, "Give me contentment." We can have contentment and ease our personal pain if we take into account the things we hold dear. Be sure to count such things as love, friendship, and gratitude (true necessities). Let us count our blessings, and make the good seem greater until it really does become greater. Then we'll posses the contentment for which Agur longed.

Walking the path of wisdom . . .

1. Are there some areas of your life where you failed to see the good and dwelled on the negative instead?
2. What are some of the "credits" in your life? What could you do to remind yourself of these credits when the debits become overwhelming?
3. What are some ways you could change your perspective on your circumstances this week? What could you do to see the "equity"?

77.

Make Your Means Right Regardless of the End

All of a person's ways seem right to him, but God weighs a person's intentions (Proverbs 16:2).

Sometimes we pursue a course of action that may not be right, but we deem it *right* because it will get us what we want (but God is not fooled). Jacob, one of the Hebrew patriarchs, illustrates this misguided approach.*

Eager for gain, Jacob dupes his brother, Esau, into giving up his birthright. Jacob carries the deception further and tricks his father, Isaac, into giving him the blessing of the first-born. Esau, furious at getting a second-rate fate, seeks to kill his brother.

Jacob has to flee to Haran. Still, he doesn't learn his lesson. Over a period of twenty years, Jacob hustles his way into obtaining wives, servants, children, and cattle. Eventually, he decides to return to Canaan. He travels as far as the River Jabok when someone suddenly attacks him. He wrestles the whole night with the unknown assailant. As morning nears, Jacob is prevailing. But suddenly, with just a touch, the attacker dislodges Jacob's hip. Immediately, Jacob realizes that he has not been wrestling with any ordinary man but with an agent of God.

Jacob has sought blessing his whole life, often getting his gains by less-than-admirable means, and now he seeks a blessing from this unknown being. No doubt Jacob has in mind the land promised to him by his father's blessing, but before Jacob can take possession of the land, God considers something else necessary—a new character must take hold of Jacob.

The name Jacob means *deceiver*, and as an admission of guilt, the agent of God asks Jacob for his name. Jacob confesses his name and thereby confesses his flawed approach to living—getting gains by any means. Jacob, hobbled and humbled by God, now possesses the right nature to receive a divine blessing.

What do we learn from Jacob? Any end, regardless of how noble, is denigrated if the means are not equally noble. Contrary to the popular saying, the end never justifies the means. Furthermore, when we seek gain by questionable means, we compromise our character. Our nature shrivels, and we become less than worthy of the very things that we achieve or acquire (God is not fooled). If we acquire with proper means, we will also garner a noble character, which has an even greater value than our intended end.

Walking the path of wisdom . . .

1. Why do you think Jacob chose deception rather than an honest way of getting ahead? Why do you do what you do? Do you know your own intentions?
2. Is there any situation in which a person could legitimately condone any means to achieve an end?
3. Have you ever gained something by less than noble means? What was the outcome?

NOTES:

* Nearly everyone wants a life rich in what he considers valuable—maybe that's material possessions, a brood of happy children, or a life full of love. The Hebrew patriarch Jacob demonstrates the lengths a person may go to find abundance in an austere world. If you find, like Jacob, your life is short on the blessings for which you long, read the free article, *Beware the Touch of God*. Also check out the free article, *The Power of a Paradigm*. Both are available at the resource page: www.ThePathofWisdom.com/resources.htm.

78.

Don't Be Afraid to Discipline Your Children

Train up a child in the way he should go, and when he is old, he will not depart from it (Proverbs 22:6).

Developmental psychologists, not to mention the sages of *Proverbs*, tell us that our character takes shape in our early years. It's far wiser to shape a child while young than to wait for a child to grow into his ways. However, parents, grandparents, and guardians often fear giving correction and instruction, lest they impinge upon the child's dignity or ruin his self-esteem. But it's possible for parents to provide discipline that both corrects behavior and preserves dignity.

Preserve a child's dignity by refusing to demean him or her. Children are thinking, feeling human beings, but frequently adults speak to them as lesser just because they are younger or smaller. Some adults have a tendency to be rude to children, using tones they would not use with an adult. Just as boys and girls are expected to treat adults and other kids with respect and courtesy, adults need to treat children the same way.

Preserve a child's dignity by avoiding actions that would embarrass the child. If we reprimand a child in front of others, we are not helping him. We are actually demoralizing him. Publicly reprimanding a child accentuates his faults. A better method would be to correct the child in private, and this would also help the child to put his "best foot forward."

Preserve a child's dignity by offering choices. Provide a child with options. For example, if a child exhibits poor behavior at the dinner table, parents tend to say, "Do what I say—or else." A contrasting approach, however, would offer a choice, "You can finish your dinner, and then you can have dessert. Or, if you don't want to finish your dinner, you can get down and go to your room." Choices like these are especially important during the teen years.

Preserve a child's dignity by explaining the reasons for what you expect. The often-used phrase, "Because I said so," fails to provide a reason. Offering reasons does not diminish the parent's authority, but reinforces it. When a child knows why something should be done, he or she is empowered to do it in the future.

The success or failure of the next generation, perhaps the next two generations, hinges on the kind of discipline they receive. But training a child in the right path can be painful work, requiring persistence and patience. While a parent's efforts may be a source of grief in the short-term, setting a child's course headlong toward character and prosperity will bring joy in the long-term—*he will not depart from it.*

Walking the path of wisdom . . .

1. What are some ways you can effectively train a child so he or she is on the right path?
2. In your upbringing, which had the most effect: punishment and discipline, or verbal instruction and encouragement?
3. If a child strays from the way taught, what conclusions can we make about the child or about the parents (Proverbs 22:6)?

79.

Dishonesty Does You No Service

Truthfulness endures forever, but lying lasts only for the moment (Proverbs 12:19).

Lying seems to come almost as easily as breathing. One survey says that ninety-one percent of Americans routinely lie (and the other nine percent lie about not lying). When something immoral or unethical, such as lying, becomes commonplace in a society, the behavior becomes more acceptable and the consequences become progressively negligible. For instance, the permitting or fostering of lies within a society removes any apprehension associated with lying or its consequences. As a result, people will tend to lie without a second thought.

Dishonesty by definition attempts to conceal, but its effects are not hidden. Falsehood impedes the healthy development of social systems and poisons personal relationships. Lying is *for the moment*—an easy out, a short-lived solution—and the person who lies is not thinking of the long-term consequences. For instance, the lie must be repeated and maintained, and as a result, serves as a constant source of anxiety. Likewise, a person who lies may avoid ruin or shame for the time being, but he will not escape the hardening of his soul.

The best-known form of lying is when we say something opposite from what we know is fact or reality. We contradict the truth. For instance, a man lies on an auto loan if he claims two years at his current job when the fact is, he has only been there six months.

Lying also includes leaving out the truth or adding to the truth. Implying something false by not telling all, failing to speak out when someone is lying, or allowing someone to take the blame when we are to blame, are all examples of leaving out the truth.

Furthermore, we lie when we add to the truth. Whenever we elaborate on or exaggerate the facts, we lie. When we give people a different conclusion about a situation than the facts themselves would allow, again, we lie.

According to Hebrew teaching, the heart is easily self-deceived. We would thus be wise to suspect ourselves and give careful consideration to when we might be lying. Likewise, we would be wise to accept that the truth also has consequences, and these consequences are considerably more positive than those of lying. Truthful means and ways cannot help but endure. They herald inner and outer peace, as well as shape positive relationships.

Walking the path of wisdom . . .

1. What is wrong with lying? What damage does lying do?
2. Do you consider yourself an honest person? If so, do you ever catch yourself lying? How can you reconcile the two? Do you know anyone who lies frequently? If so, do you respect or trust them?
3. Have you ever been caught in a lie or hurt others by lying? Have these experiences helped you to understand the importance of telling the truth?

80.

Envy and Jealousy Eat Away at the Soul

Wrath is fierce and anger a flood, but who can stand before envy or jealousy (Proverbs 27:4).

Have you ever let your eyes wander to the reading material of someone seated next to you and thought that his magazine was more appealing than yours? Have you ever been in a restaurant and thought that the meal someone else ordered looks more appetizing than your own? These examples represent *envy* on a small scale. Our proverb warns against envy and jealousy.

Envy is stirred up by seeing the prosperity or blessing of another person and wanting it for ourselves. Can we bear it when someone passes us by? Can we take pleasure in the success of another? Admittedly, I have difficulty doing this. When someone tells me of his success, I have a hard time being happy for him. I start to ferment within and feel that I should be the one with the success. Then, I have to talk myself into a different mindset.

Just as envy can easily overwhelm a person, the same is true of jealousy. Jealousy arises when we resent what someone else has because we think we are more deserving. Can anyone stand before jealousy's torrent of emotion? Wrath and anger surge like a flash flood, but they don't compare to the passion of jealousy. Many men have wonderful wives, and admittedly, I sometimes resent their good fortune and feel that I'm more deserving of a good wife than them. Again, I have to think my way out of this powerful emotion.

The proverb alludes to how easily jealousy and envy overpower their victims, both the subject and the object. In C.S. Lewis' *Screwtape Letters*, the star called Wormwood turned all the waters it fell upon bitter. Similarly, jealousy and envy poison anything enjoyable or refreshing in a person's life. Furthermore, since the envious or jealous person can't stand the thought of his neighbor's advantage, he may look for pleasure in his neighbor's ruin. By trickery, gossip, and any other petty instrument in jealousy's arsenal, he might attempt to bring about his neighbor's downfall.

Happiness does not come by comparing ourselves to others. Let's get what we can from our own magazine or meal—from our own life. If our lives are full, we won't feel envious or jealous of what others possess. Besides, the thing we desire that belongs to another might not fit or agree with us (even if we could get it). Let us live so intently, so abundantly, that the joy we possess takes joy in the rewards and blessings of others.

Walking the path of wisdom . . .

1. Are you genuinely thankful for what God has given you? Or is your gratitude subject to how you compare to others?
2. Are you happy for others when they succeed or are blessed? How does this manifest itself?
3. Do you consider yourself a jealous or envious person? If so, why do you think you're that way, and what can you do about it?

81.

To Hear Wisdom's Call: Practice Stillness

Wisdom says, "Blessed is the person who listens to me, watching daily at my gates, waiting at my foyer. Anyone who finds me finds life" (Proverbs 8:34, 35).

Genuine peace, satisfaction, and blessing come by listening for wisdom, *waiting* and *watching* daily at her gates. Unfortunately, we are not given to this kind of stillness. Instead, we prefer perpetual activity. This is never more evident than in our unceasing thoughts. Stilling our minds is necessary to hear and discern the voice of wisdom, which is not easily heard. We need to do some kind of *watching* to develop our awareness.

One solution is to practice a biofeedback exercise, one that draws your attention away from your ordinary flow of thoughts to a more quiet state. First, find a place and time that is relatively quiet. This way you won't be disturbed by excessive noise. Next, find a comfortable position so that you won't be thinking about your body. And since you can think on what you see, close your eyes too. Now, for a minute or two, focus solely on your breathing. Consciously take notice of each breath as you inhale and exhale.

The next step is to begin to still your thoughts. Choose a special word (one or two syllables) that makes you feel at ease. Now, each time you recognize that you're thinking about something, gently place the word in your awareness but not on your lips. This use of your special word reduces ordinary casual thoughts by reaffirming your intention to interior silence.

When the exercise becomes a habit, you will usually have about a minute and a half of inner quiet before you need to return to the word. There are times, however, when your mind will wander from start to finish. Even when that happens, the exercise is still valuable in helping you create inner calm.

You can turn this biofeedback exercise into a spiritual exercise, called centering prayer.* Make the word a sacred word, somehow related to your personal religious or spiritual beliefs, and make the intent not only that of interior silence, but also union with the divine. My sacred word is *Father*, and my intent is union with God the Father, waiting and watching before him.

The ultimate purpose of this exercise, whether biofeedback or centering prayer, is not merely waiting, but the integration of silence with the daily tasks of living—making our days more blessed. By stillness we avail ourselves to the deeper waters of our person, and perhaps to the divine as well, where we hear and receive wisdom to enrich life with greater peace.

Walking the path of wisdom . . .

1. Would your inner life be more accurately described as chaotic or tranquil? Why?
2. Are you willing to deliberately set apart time every day to still your heart and mind? Why or why not?
3. What obstacles do you need to overcome in order to remove yourself from the noise and activity of life?

NOTES:

* Centering prayer is such a crucial component to experiencing wisdom that I'm making available the article, *Centering Prayer: Journey to Divine Union*. It will guide you in practicing this enriching spiritual discipline. In centering prayer, you don't just modify your thoughts or change your life, rather, God, the Divine, transforms you—and there's no experience so amazing. Find it among other free resources: www.ThePathofWisdom.com/resources.htm.

82.

Correcting Others Is Sometimes Necessary

Whoever rebukes a person will in the end gain more favor than someone with a flattering tongue (Proverbs 28:23).

Giving correction can be difficult for some people (including me), most likely because we fear a defensive or hostile reaction. In an attempt to evade conflict, we might resort to stalling, avoidance, flattery, or some other defense mechanism. Other people, however, may have no problem confronting. But the manner in which some people confront may not be constructive. As a result, they can't expect a favorable outcome.

If we confront people constructively and graciously, initially others might respond defensively (or worse), but most people will eventually acquiesce and appreciate the correction. Here are some suggestions for giving helpful criticism:

State your positive intent. If you're like me, you probably don't tell your intent up front; we simply assume others know our intention. Ironically, this is the most important part of correcting. Ask yourself beforehand, "What is my purpose for saying what I'm going to say? What result would I like to see?" And communicate this to the other person.

Check your tone of voice. Even if you intend well, an angry, defensive, or condescending tone of voice alerts people to ignore your words and respond to the tone. If you notice that your tone implies something different than your words, then defuse the tone by explaining it. For instance: "I know I sound angry, but that's just because the issue is so important to me." By so doing, you decrease the likelihood of someone reacting to your tone.

Tactfully interrupt interruptions. If the other person interrupts, yells, curses, or becomes aggressive, gently repeat the person's name or title until he ceases. "Excuse me, Sir. Uh, Sir. Sir.

Pardon me, Sir." Repeating the name or title has a way of derailing the person from his hurtful course. Once you have regained his attention, continue your point, restate your intent, or clarify what he is mishearing.

Be specific about the problem or error. Be careful not to blame or label the person as the problem, and be on guard against exaggerations such as "always" and "never." Instead, point out the behavior at issue. Cite specific examples when appropriate.

Without room for rebuke in an association, friendship, or bond, it's hard to believe the relationship is based on anything substantive. As much as we may want to avoid giving criticism, it is an important part of effective associations and loving relationships, provided it's done in a friendly or loving manner. Honest and gracious correction is much more meaningful than saccharine politeness or harsh blame.

Walking the path of wisdom . . .

1. Why do you think it's important to give criticism in a healthy relationship? Have you ever received a less than kind correction? How did you react?
2. How do you give correction? Do you offer correction in the heat of the moment? Are you conscious of your attitude and motives?
3. Is there someone you may need to confront this week? Why? How?

83.

Don't Let Your Fears Control You

A fearful heart weighs a person down, but kind words may lighten the load (Proverbs 12:25).

When we experience a traumatic event at any age—a bee sting, a dog bite, a fall, a failure at public speaking—it triggers unpleasant emotions. The depth of our fear of bees, dogs, heights, public speaking, etc., is a consequence of those unpleasant experiences—we don't want to repeat them. But the more we attempt to avoid them, the more ingrained the fear becomes.

Fear can cause the reaction of inaction. Somehow, somewhere we came to accept that fear was an acceptable excuse for inaction—*a fearful heart weighs a person down*. We can live that way if we choose, but it will be a life that misses out, a life devoid of great success, or a life given to the mundane. We're better off confronting our fears.

When you find yourself in a fearful situation, instead of becoming caught up in the fear, make a conscious effort to think through the situation and visualize a positive outcome. First, tell yourself that these feelings are related to past events and have little or nothing to do with the current problem. Next, imagine yourself overcoming your fear and successfully handling the situation. Last, and this is the most important step, whatever the situation or fear—will yourself to do it.

The best way to get over long held fears or phobias is to face the initiating experience directly. Make a list of every fear you have, then close your eyes and point to the list. Open your eyes. Wherever your finger points, that's your first fear to overcome. Repeatedly confront the fear until it no longer controls you. Conquering your fears can be exciting if you face them with this method.

Instead of facing the actual situation, you could confront the fear or phobia in your mind; this is called a mind movie. While not as effective as facing the fearful event directly, a mind movie can still be helpful. Find a quiet place to sit and close your eyes. Repeatedly envision yourself going through the fear-triggering situation, handling it successfully and without fear. For instance, you could use this process before going into a meeting or a negotiation, and picture yourself without fear—confident, communicating well, and getting the deal you want.

You're controlled by what you fear, but you can render your fears powerless. When you confront your fears, you will typically find that they're nothing like the negative outcome you had imagined. Then they will no longer have dominion, and you can live more freely and take on greater challenges.

Walking the path of wisdom . . .

1. Does fear control any area of your life? If so, what specifically do you fear? How have these fears impacted your life?
2. Have you ever tried to overcome these fears? Were you successful? Are you willing to employ the suggestions above?
3. Can you picture yourself handling your fearful situation successfully? Or can you face the fear directly?

84.

Let the Words of Another Praise You

The crucible is for silver and the furnace for gold, and a person is tested by the praise accorded him (Proverbs 27:21, NIV).

Praise can have the sound of sweet music or a totally out of tune instrument. If the praise comes from someone else, then it sounds in tune to all whom hear it. This is not the case when the praise comes from one's own mouth. Self-adulation has a way of creating dissonance in the ears of the hearers. Nothing lowers a person more in the view of his peers than when he sings his own praises.

Most people who flatter themselves despise it when other people praise themselves. For that matter, no one likes to hear someone's self-adulation. Thus, for the most part, self-seeking accomplishes the opposite of the seeker's intent. Instead of bringing him recognition, it brings him dishonor.

It would be wise to watch carefully what we say about ourselves. Perhaps we speak of what we truly are, but the temptation to portray ourselves as more is great. Instead, let our works and not our tongues commend us (Proverbs 31:31). Our name will not suffer loss if we keep our mouths quiet regarding ourselves.

If someone is praised by others, the praised person not only receives approval but is also proven. Adulation tests a person's character as much any reproach. If the person is usually humble, then maybe he won't be moved to arrogance. But if the person is typically vain, then he will probably surrender to self-importance. In this case, the commended person shows that his character is not sufficient to handle praise's allure.

Undoubtedly, anyone offering adulation has good intentions, but he places a potential poison before the person he praises. And it's difficult for the praised person to avoid taking a drop, even subconsciously. If someone praises you, receive it cautiously—with gratitude or self-renouncement. Here's one specific way to carefully accept commendation: Let it be known that others also deserve the credit.

The *furnace* of praise tests the metal of a person. Put the finest person in the fire, and notice how much dross is still present, notice how much refining is still needed. If a person will humble herself, the *crucible* of praise will remove the dross—flaws like haughtiness and arrogance. The person humbled by praise realizes how little she deserves it; she knows she is still in need of purifying.

Walking the path of wisdom . . .

1. What is the problem with "tooting your own horn"?
2. What dangers should we be aware of when it comes to talking about ourselves? What dangers should we be aware of when others praise us?
3. How might avoiding self-adulation actually gain us greater appreciation and praise from others?

85.

Make Sure Your Wealth Counts

The house of those who live rightly has much wealth, but those who handle their income poorly find sorrow (Proverbs 15:6).

How often do we hear of people who have much but are not happy? Adding riches can mean adding sorrows. One reason may be that those who have much do not put their wealth to its best use. When utilized properly, riches do not lead to sorrow but result in joy. The following uses reflect a wise and rewarding approach to riches (although some people may consider these uses improper).

Riches may be wisely used for positive influence. Many people love the rich (Proverbs 14:20). How the rich live, where they dine, what are their getaway spots—these are of great interest to some people. These admirers of the rich are subject to the influence that the rich and wealthy wield. People who are wealthy *and* wise employ this influence ethically and use it to advance a greater good, their own good as well as that of others.

Riches may be wisely used to enjoy life. Much of our culture has a slavish preoccupation with success. Anyone obsessed with having more success or wealth will fail to enjoy what he has already achieved or gained. But this need not be true of the rich. Since they have plenty, they can take the attitude that enjoying what they have is more beneficial than getting more. The wise take time to enjoy the blessings of their prosperity.

Riches may be wisely used in investments. There is one who scatters (as in scattering seeds) yet increases all the more (Proverbs 11:24). When someone scatters his wealth in wise investments, it results in even greater riches. The unwise scatter what they have in ruinous speculations, and as a result, they lose what they have. Anyone who wants to keep or increase his wealth will need to learn how to invest sensibly.*

The meaning of *much wealth* is not limited to money or possessions but includes contentment and satisfaction (Proverbs 10:22). Many rich people are dissatisfied and unhappy, which means they are not truly wealthy. Some poor people are happy and content, which means they are wealthier than they know. Evidently, it's possible for those with much to live in sorrow, while people with little live happily. It all depends upon the attitude and practices of the household.

There's treasure and increase in the home that uses their income wisely. Let's make the most of our money and possessions; let's be among the wise.

See also entries 45, 46, 49, and 79.

Walking the path of wisdom . . .

1. What is the relationship between wisdom and wealth? Does wealth necessarily produce wisdom? Does wisdom necessarily produce wealth?
2. Are your possessions and wealth a source of joy or sorrow? Describe.
3. How do you use that which God has given you? How can wealth be used legitimately to better yourself and your family?

* Two effective strategies for wise investment include fundamentals trading and swing trading. To learn more about one or both of these approaches check out www.thepathofwisdom.com/resources.htm.

86.

The Mouth Speaks What Is in the Heart

Guard your heart with all diligence, for the heart is the wellspring of life. Put perversity far from your mouth, and keep corrupt talk far from your lips (Proverbs 4:23–24).

The most important part of both body and soul is the heart. It is the vital spring of life, whether naturally or spiritually. The heart is the citadel of a person, the fountain of actions, the seat of principle, the place of character, and also the dwelling of corruption. From these depths flow the deeds of life, and nowhere is this more evident than with what gushes from the *mouth*.

Whatever is in the heart, the well of life, will determine the nature of the words that spring forth. A person with decency in her heart will most often use positive language. Conversely, a person with *perversity* in her heart will bring forth malice in her speech.

A wellspring of water will usually run deep beneath the surface before it springs forth. Similarly, a wellspring in a person will typically rise from a person's depths and flow outward.* We can increase the good waters at the depths of our person by intentionally guarding our hearts.

We guard our hearts by watching what we say. Speaking in corruptible ways—such as grumbling, cursing, and half-truths—shapes habits of thought. Yes, words form thoughts as much as thoughts form words. The words we utter become flesh within us; we become what we say. If we avoid corrupt speech, we avoid making corruption a part of our person. Similarly, if we use constructive words to express a matter, we will instill goodness deep in the heart. There the good words are stored and available for access.

We guard our hearts by watching what we see. It has been said that the eye is the window to the soul. We can almost determine what resides deep within some people by looking into their eyes. Similarly, what we see has a way entering through the eyes and proceeding deep into our souls. If we make a habit of watching what is violent or pornographic, these perversions will find their way into our souls and overflow in our behavior and speech.

The nature of a person's inner-self will determine the nature of his acts, and this includes the words he speaks. Watch the heart. Guard the fountain, so that the waters don't become poisoned. Eventually, the well deep within will consist of only good words, and these words will naturally flow from your person.

See also entry 64.

Walking the path of wisdom . . .

1. Do you ever reflect on the nature and content of your heart? If so, what is the state of your heart?
2. Do you see a parallel between the nature of your heart and the content of your speech? What is involved in guarding the heart?
3. Are you willing to purify your heart by meditating upon what is true, noble, pure, admirable, and praiseworthy? Do you believe this would make a difference?

NOTES:

* Jesus the great wisdom teacher put it this way, "People don't pick grapes from thorn bushes or figs from thistles. Similarly, good fruit comes only from good trees, and a rotten tree is sure to produce bad fruit" (Matthew 7:17).

87.

Glitz and Glamour Are Not Necessarily Gold

A beautiful woman who lacks discretion is like a gold jewel in a pig's snout (Proverbs 11: 22).

In contrast to the American dream of the past, many people have reduced today's dream to that of becoming a star—an admired one, even if being a star means a quick burn out. These bright lights, however, are nothing more than corrupted symbols of success and glory.

We know the expression, "Not all that glitters is gold," and this is never truer than when it comes to glitz and glamour. Many want to shine in the manufactured light of the TV or big screen, but that light shines only for a moment then fades like the flickering at the end of a film.

The pursuit of glitz, glamour, and glory are attempts to be valued as *beautiful* in some manner or another. While most cultures value beauty, the Hebrew sage does so with this caveat: attractiveness without discretion is vanity. Those who pursue glitz may be externally beautiful, but if that's the only beauty they pursue —they lack discretion and gain vanity. While their appearance may be admired by some people, their external adornment amounts to little more than a gold jewel in a pig's snout.

People who take pride in their appearance consider their status to be an indicator of their value and worth (e.g., some elitists and many Hollywood celebrities), but little do they know, they are actually covered in disgrace. The obsession with one's appearance before others, the capture of desired objects, the subtle allure of indiscriminate pleasure—these pursuits may be cherished as if they're gold, but they are little more than rubbish.

Of course, any person of glamour or status who hears this conclusion will consider it ridiculous. Surrounded by people who are likewise self-deceived, they encourage each other in their ongoing vanity or extravagance.

Many people admire the things that supposedly fill these beautiful people, but given their pitiable character and sometimes their dreaded end, they do not warrant admiration (Proverbs 24:1–2). The glitz seekers may fool much of the world, but those with eyes to see know that the way of glitz leads to a superfluous life.

Wisdom prefers to value something more than external ornaments. Many people have removed self-denial, self-restraint, personal responsibility, and similar attributes from the alter of admired qualities. But when a person of *discretion* pursues these traits or anything truly admirable—she adorns her soul.

Walking the path of wisdom . . .

1. What is wrong with the pursuit of glitz and glamour?
2. Do you feel you have eyes to see the danger of glitz and glamour? Do you ever find yourself giving in to the allure of glitz and glamour?
3. What can you do to limit an over-emphasis on external adornments in your life and pursue more noble qualities?

88.

Use Well Humanity's Tendency to Worship

The fear of the Lord is a fountain of life, turning a man from the snares of death (Proverbs 14: 27, NIV).

The Hebrews distinguished humans from the rest of the creatures in this world by something called the "image of God." Perhaps the meaning of the expression lies in our capacity to exceed animals in self-awareness, rational thinking, and intentional love. But here is another possible connotation: Just as God glories in himself, God's image in humanity glories in self and others. In other words, intrinsic to humanity is a need to offer or receive praise, adulation, or worship.

All humans will inevitably worship something. The nations surrounding ancient Israel exemplified this tendency. Consider the Greek sculptures, where man is portrayed as the noblest of all creatures. And what about Egypt or Babylon? Their worship included objects such as bulls, birds, dogs, and the like. They could not help but worship something.

Similarly, take a look at the things we venerate: celebrities who flaunt their disdain for what is good and decent; expensive toys to which we give our attention and service (e.g., incessantly waxing the Mercedes); sports teams that we fervently follow and cheer. Still other people worship their portfolio; that is, they give their ultimate affection to their investments. Each day, they exercise as much devotion or anxiety as did any ancient person in going to the Temple of Zeus or the Temple of Yahweh.

The key to understanding worship as *Proverbs* expects is found in the repeated refrain: *the fear of the Lord*. The word *fear* refers to a wonder or admiration caused by something or someone grand. If you have ever met an admired sports figure or movie star, you know this feeling. You swell with emotion, seemingly without control. Our sage says that we should have this kind of awe for the Lord—for God.

Given that humans possess the image of God, it's understandable that we would worship other humans, but since this worship begins and ends with humans, it is worship only of the image and not the originator of the image. This worship of humans (or anything less than us), and not the originator, actually denigrates our humanity. If we fail to recognize from whence we come, then we make ourselves less than we are. Conversely, when we honor the origin of our being, we become more fully human.

The songbird naturally sings in honor to its creator, but we humans must choose our worship. We can worship something lesser or something greater—and nothing is greater than God. Let's cease the worship of anything that does not dignify our humanity and choose to worship what really matters—chiefly God.

Walking the path of wisdom . . .

1. "All humans will inevitably worship something." Agree or disagree? Why?
2. How do we make ourselves less than fully human when we do what is in essence the worship of other humans?
3. In what ways can we worship the originator of our humanity? What effect might this have on our lives?

89.

Purpose Is More Fulfilling Than Pleasure

A person who lacks understanding delights in pleasure, but a person with a sensible purpose keeps a straight course (Proverbs 15:21).

Pleasure is the gratification of our desires, but rarely do our desires remain satisfied. The satisfaction passes. This fact does not make pleasure meaningless, but it does mean that we should recognize pleasure for what it is—a temporary gratification. Pleasure cannot suffice as something lasting—for that we need *purpose*. Pleasure is fleeting, but purpose is enduring.

Although purpose is more lasting than pleasure, not every purpose holds equal significance. Some people think knowledge is a great purpose. While *Proverbs* is full of admonitions to obtain knowledge, the person who sets knowledge as his primary focus never quite arrives. After all, "knowing is largely a means of discovering the greatness of one's ignorance" (*Quiet Talks on Personal Problems*, 89).

Some people believe money to be a grand pursuit. True, money can enormously increase the possible power of a person, but since money is fleeting (Proverbs 23:4–5), it cannot satisfy as a lasting end.

Still others think that achievement makes for a great ultimate end. They may be onto something. Anyone who aspires to some noble accomplishment aims higher than knowledge or money. When the union of body, mind, and spirit in some noble effort inspires the soul to attain the unattainable, then aspiration has fashioned the finest in a person. The person of noble ambition makes herself largely what she wills (in conjunction with God and his sovereignty).

The person of noble ambition indeed soars high, but there's one aspiration that takes a person even higher. The utmost purpose is mastery over the inner person—the pursuit of an ever improving character. We advance in character through the addition and enhancement of positive attributes but also through attempts to bring passion and pleasure under control. Anyone who rules his own tendencies toward self-gratification, bringing them under subjection, has attained more than the greatest rulers of the world, most of whom have little self-mastery.

Purpose is more enduring and satisfying than pleasure. Scum may settle at the bottom of the cup of pleasure, and those who drink deeply may make themselves ill. But the cup of purpose is always full to the brim with what is life-giving. Purpose unites the separate days of our lives by a thread of continuity and keeps us on a *straight* and fulfilling *course*.

Walking the path of wisdom . . .

1. Are your pursuits primarily driven by a desire for pleasure? Why? Have you ever pursued pleasure and felt unsatisfied? How can you gain mastery over these tendencies toward self-gratification?
2. Are your life's pursuits meaningful and enduring? If not, are you willing to re-evaluate? Do you have some noble ambitions you should pursue?
3. What are your most important pursuits? How can you purse the ambition of a noble character?

90.

You're Responsible for What You Believe

There is a path that seems right to a person, but its end is the way of death (Proverbs 14:12).

According to this proverb, a person determines the outcome of his life by the *path* he chooses. A person may follow a path *that seems right* but is actually wrong, and should he persist in this wrong way, he will end up where he did not expect—he will perish.

On *the way of death*, vice passes as virtue, envy is considered good, and death is mistaken for life. Soon enough, though, the disguise falls away and the person discovers, usually too late, that the outcome is not what he expected. And no amount of belief in his path's rightness will change the inevitable and unexpected outcome.

A person's opinion that a way is right does not make it right, and sincerity in a faulty belief will not exempt someone from the unexpected result. For instance, a person purchases what he thinks is a solid stock, but no amount of sincerity, regardless of his favorable opinion, will prevent a loss if the stock is unstable. The tumbling price will prove his opinion false and his sincerity inadequate. Accordingly, a hollow philosophy of life deceives people into thinking that sincerity matters more than believing the right thing. What a person believes matters. One must make sure *the way* is right.

The way refers to your perception of reality and your subsequent choices and actions. You are the only person responsible for what you believe and the outcome of those beliefs. Sure, to some extent your beliefs have been shaped by your past (the story of your life) and influenced by the culture (the prevailing beliefs of the day), but only you can examine and test those beliefs against the possible outcomes. Only you can ask the question: Is my belief system bringing me greater life or producing what can only be construed as death (literal or metaphorical)? The more aware you are of your beliefs, the more likely you'll be able to shift any deadly beliefs to what is life-affirming.*

The effect of your beliefs is this: In them you will arrive at an outcome you desired or an outcome you did not expect. You owe it to yourself to examine your beliefs and determine, given your present course, what is your eventual destination. Regardless of what the world thinks, there is a way that is right, and this wise path ends in life. That's the path you want to be on.

Walking the path of wisdom . . .

1. Do you agree that your beliefs say a lot about what you can expect out of life? Why or why not?
2. What's the problem with clinging to the notion that a person needs to only be sincere in his or her beliefs?
3. Are you willing to examine your beliefs to see where they are taking you? If not, why?

NOTES:

* Generally speaking, a person's beliefs set a course for life that will result in either fulfillment or despondency. Anything wielding that much power and influence over person's potential happiness should be carefully examined. If you want to reevaluate your beliefs, and where they might be taking you, one possible tool to assist you is the article, *The Power of a Paradigm*, free at my resource page: www.ThePathofWisdom.com/resources.htm.

91.

Stop Running From Wisdom's Pursuit

How long will the simple pursue their ways? Wisdom shouts in the streets; she lifts her voice in the public square. "Turn to my leading, and behold, I will pour out my spirit on you" (Proverbs 1:20, 22, 23).

Wisdom shouts in the streets and cries out in the public places, attempting to attract the attention of those eagerly pursing their own course. Wisdom wishes to lay hold of us, but we ridicule her and pursue our own way. Wisdom's call to forgive those who wrong us, to possess gratitude for our problems, or to put others before ourselves (just to name a few) sounds ridiculous, and we opt instead for what we know—the world's way.

Wisdom calls for us to turn to her leading, and we *turn* by trust. To express the word *trust*, the ancient Hebrews used the term *batach*, which conveys the idea of helplessly lying face down. One can lie on his back, as one does when looking at the stars, and from that position he can quickly rise if threatened. Or one can lay prostrate face down and arms outstretched, as one does when being arrested, and from that position he is vulnerable. We take the vulnerable position in one of two situations: when commanded to under threat or when we feel completely safe. The key to trusting wisdom is this: Can we come to feel safe lying prostrate before her?

Wisdom is presented in these verses as a person—a female. In the Hebrew tradition, God is also presented in personal terms, but usually in masculine language. Given the close association in *Proverbs* between God and the woman wisdom, it could be that wisdom is the feminine side of God.* But to lie helplessly before anyone, including God, is contrary to our enculturation. Whether we will trust God depends on whether we feel we can put ourselves in a vulnerable position before him (or his feminine side).

You may not realize it, but the feminine side of God is worthy of your vulnerability. The woman wisdom, this feminine side of God, possesses all the attributes that she suggests others follow. She is fundamentally good, and in her goodness, she wishes to pour out her spirit upon (bless) anyone who turns to her. In other words, it's safe to lie face down before her.

Giving up your own path is difficult, especially if you feel God (or his feminine side) has wronged you in the past. I understand the resistance that accompanies such a *turn*. I have faced it too. But without a turn to God and his ways, you will miss wisdom's best for you. Despite assumptions or experiences, wisdom's ways are not a hindrance. They are the path of blessing.

Walking the path of wisdom . . .

1. Is your life characterized by inner turmoil, or do you possess a sense of peace? Describe.
2. Have you ever had the sense that something or someone is calling you to a different kind of life? Can you describe this inner call? Did you respond?
3. Do you believe living wisely can be fulfilling, or do you tend to believe that such an approach to life removes pleasure and spontaneity? Why?

NOTES:

* Wisdom might be the feminine side of God, but whoever Wisdom is, she calls out to humanity, offering gifts more valuable than silver and gold. Regardless whether these gifts are metaphorical or literal, it be valuable to know who this person is and how we might meet her. *Meet the Incarnation of Wisdom* in the free article at: www.ThePathofWisdom.com/resources.htm.

92.

Accept Where You Are

There is surely a future hope for you, and your hope will not be cut off (Proverbs 23:18, NIV).

Human nature is such that a person tends to look upon his failures as the sum of his life, but berating self for how life has turned out accomplishes nothing. Where you are, is where you are. The past is forever closed. No amount of dwelling on it can change the present, and no amount of self-flagellation can make you something different.

Typically, we compare ourselves to the world's standard of success and fret over our perceived shortcomings. Whether we come up short in the pursuit of something good or succeed in doing something wrong, it does not make us failures. It makes us human.

Do not sever your *future hope*. Take a moment to tell yourself that where you are at in this point of life is acceptable, no matter what your failings or circumstances.

A person should live as if her whole existence were narrowed down to this very day, with no useless regret for the past and no useless worry for the future. She should live this day as if it were her only day—the only day for her to assert all that is best in her, the only day left for her to conquer all that is worst in her.

Imagine a slippery, moss-covered rock protruding slightly from a fast-flowing river. Now, picture yourself standing on that rock. In front of you are similar stones, and the only way to cross the rapid stream is to step one rock at a time. You may not like your location, but your only point of balance lies on the rock beneath you. No amount of griping about your current predicament will change the fact that you are where you are—on a slippery stone, in a dicey predicament. Your best chance of being somewhere else is simply to accept where you stand and slowly, persistently take one sure step at a time, rock by rock. With each step, comes the assurance of a future hope.

We expect results from ourselves, but since results may lie outside our control, they are not the best test of true living. Whether success or failure, there is but one question to bravely and honestly ask yourself, "How will this current condition affect me?" Will the situation make you truer, better, or nobler? The answer is determined entirely by you.

Our proverb has the weight of divine assurance. By God's help, let's turn our past failures and wasted opportunities into hope and confidence for now and the future.

See also entries 20 and 24.

Walking the path of wisdom . . .

1. Are there some things from your past that you need to let go of in order to move on with your life? How will you let them go?
2. Do you believe that making the most of every day can radically change your present and your future? How?
3. Do you strive every day to improve your life (e.g., use your time more wisely, think more positively, or help others more freely)? What are some simple steps you can take to move ahead stone by stone?

93.

Become What You Wish to Be: Act as if

Once the whirlwind passes, those who delight in living wrongly will be gone, but those who consistently do rightly will be established forever (Proverbs 10:25).

Many people, including me, are dissatisfied with who they are or how they act. But wherever a person is in his character; he is not limited in what he may become. He can become something more, better, or different; he can become something stronger, surer, or steadier.

The best a person may become lies within her own heart, mind, and soul, and while her potential may not come forth easily, she can manifest it by will and practice.* The way to establish yourself as a person of character and integrity, a stabilizing force who can't be moved even by a whirlwind, is to *consistently do rightly.* William James, one of the first self-improvement authors, put it his way: "If you want a quality, act as if you already have it."

Act as if. You have probably heard these three words before. If we take the most obvious meaning, there is no great mystery: Act as if you already are what you want to be. What quality do you want to possess? Get that image in your mind, then act as though you already have it, even when (especially when) you don't feel like it.

By acting as if, you're seeking to become what you want to be by reinforcing the behaviors that will get you there. For instance, do you wish to be a healthier person? What would that person do? What would she eat? How often would she exercise? That's what you do now and tomorrow.

The reward for this intentional role-playing comes when you see that you're no longer acting but that you have grown into the new quality or identity. Act as if, moment by moment, and sooner than you may think, you won't be acting anymore. You will have become what you wanted to become—established as that person forever.

The emptiness of living according to our baser selves should move us out of our complacency and enable us to see the wonderful vision of what we can become. This present reality is too short for our vast individual and collective possibilities to be fully realized.† But let's realize all we can while we may—the whirlwinds are coming.

Walking the path of wisdom . . .

1. What qualities do you admire in others? Do you see these in yourself?
2. Have you ever tried to improve yourself and failed? Succeeded? Was there a difference in your approach?
3. Is there any area of your life that you would like to change today? If so, are you willing to live as if you've already changed?

NOTES:

* Real or transformative change can be elusive, even for people with a serious commitment to change. Why? Unhealthy beliefs and thoughts govern our actions. Changing the way we view ourselves and our reality is essential to lasting change. *Affirming the Path* will assist you in creating the right inner framework for living out the principles and practices of *The Path of Wisdom*. Find the article free at: www.ThePathofWisdom.com/resources.htm.

† The sense of incompleteness we experience in this life, regardless of the heights we may reach in our inner nature, is a strong reason for the belief in a life after this earthly one.

94.

Presume Upon Life, and You May Get Bitten

In his heart, a man assumes his course, but it is God that determines his steps (Proverbs 16:9).

From ages past, people have thought that if a person lives rightly, life (or God) will be good to him, and the Hebrews were no different in their thinking. They often considered a person's goodness to be measured in terms of material prosperity. They found it easy to see how right living *must* lead to riches. We are not so different from the Hebrews. We expect certain results out of life, and we might even think such results are due to us.

Some parts of *Proverbs* seem to suggest a formula for getting positive results. For instance, one verse says that the hopes of those who live wrongly come to nothing, but the prospect of those who live rightly is joyfulness (10:28). This verse seems to say that if we live the right way, we will have a joyful life. However, we should be careful of taking sayings like this as guarantees that doing the right things will get results.

Humans operate in a reality with many contingencies and dependencies. There is a degree of arrogance in presuming upon life—a lack of awareness as to our status as creatures. If there is one thing that wisdom teaches, it's that nothing *must* conform to our expectations. When we honestly look at reality and our own experience, we can see that some expectations have gone unmet and some formulas have failed.

A formulaic approach to life is bound to disappoint. A person who *assumes his course* is sure to be frustrated each step on the way. We think that if we do things the right way, they will invariably lead to success. Then when the success we expected doesn't happen, we feel cheated by life (or God).

Somewhere, somehow we learned that life is supposed to be easy and problem free, so when problems come, we have a hard time making sense of them. After all, it's not what we were expecting. We question God and ask why, but as the old country song suggests: We're never promised a rose garden (*Rose Garden* by Lynn Anderson).

Man proposes, but God disposes, or as the proverb puts it: Man assumes his course, but God determines his steps. Those who act according to a presumptive approach to life will eventually fall (Proverbs 16:18), succumbing to inevitable disappointment. And with every self-assured step, they actually increase the certainty and perplexity of their disappointment.

See also entries 34 and 72.

Walking the path of wisdom . . .

1. How do you measure success in life? Is it tied to your ability to control your circumstances?
2. Are you satisfied knowing that much of life is beyond your control, or are you continuously striving to gain greater control and autonomy?
3. Do you believe peace of mind to be possible in a world that you don't control?

95.

Not Everything Is About You—Really

Whoever is first in his own cause appears to be right, until the other party steps forward to question him (Proverbs 18:17).

Within humanity, there are two driving instincts to be held in tension: self-sacrifice and self-interest. A focus on one to the exclusion of the other is probably unhealthy. On one hand, a person can love others and not himself, and the life will be sapped from him. On the other hand, one can focus on himself and forget about others, and his life will lack satisfaction. In either case, the person is at odds with one of the instincts and likely dissatisfied and unhappy.

Personal growth might be assumed to be the outcome of a focus on self, but the opposite is true. The self actually deteriorates spiritually, emotionally, and relationally. Typically, when things do not go as expected for the egocentric person, he pities himself and blames others, which is not a good recipe for personal growth or positive relationships.

Given the self-absorbed person's tendency to blame, he is also likely to make negative assumptions about people. The assumptions usually follow this thought process: So-and-so has done, thought, or said such-and-such to me or about me. Any matter that supports his side of the situation is magnified; any matter that doesn't support his position is overlooked. He is first *in his own cause*.

Admittedly, self-absorption is one of my biggest weaknesses, and whenever there is a problem, situation, or uncertainty, whether expressed or unexpressed by another party, I assume that the matter is about me. I imagine that a person's words or actions have something to do with me. Even more foolishly, I attribute thoughts to others when I have no way of knowing what they are thinking.

All of my assuming only strains relationships. Instead, I should give others "the benefit of the doubt," and assume the opposite, that they do not have something against me, unless they clearly articulate a problem. I have to remind myself, "Not everything is about me."

The solution to my self-focused assumptions is to develop an altruistic outlook. When a person practices familiar forms of altruism, like giving or serving others, it will give rise to a less familiar altruism—the conscious attempt to see matters from the other person's perspective. This new perspective will make assumptions less likely.

When a person strives to keep self-sacrifice and self-interest in harmony, she will cultivate better relationships and a healthier self. Her own life will be less likely to decline, and she'll be more likely to make allowances for others. She will be less inclined to assume that issues are about her.

Walking the path of wisdom . . .

1. Do you have a tendency to give into self-absorption? If so, does this ever lead you to think things are about you when nothing has been said to that effect?
2. Why are assumptions foolish and unproductive?
3. How would having an altruistic approach to people help with the tendency to think things are about you?

96.

Always Speak Well of Others

The words of a gossip are like a tasty morsel; they go down to a person's inmost parts (Proverbs 18:8).

People delight in listening to gossip. There's an old saying that goes, "If you can't say anything nice about someone, then sit right here next to me." Gossip is a tasty morsel, which literally means *things greedily devoured.* Once these morsels get down to the *inmost parts,* they stimulate the desire for even more. A certain power accompanies our "whispering" about others.

Sadly, a gossiping or whispering tongue comes between people and creates disharmony (Proverbs 16:28). Anyone who repeats an offense causes division among people (Proverbs 17:19). This succulent morsel may become a bitter pill that creates harsh feelings, resentment, anger, and hostility. What goes down sweet may come back up and cause all kinds of stench.

Few of us will suffer at the hands of a thief or murderer, but who is immune to the careless words of a friend or the cruel tongue of an enemy. What do we feel then? If we wouldn't want gossip done to us, why would we do it to another?

Let us not add to the burden of another by our words. Always speak well of others. If we are thinking of something less-than-nice to say, let that be our cue to do the opposite. If others are gossiping about and demeaning someone, let that be our cue to interject something positive. Admittedly, this sort of interjection is more difficult for some than for others, but when it's done, it usually ends the gossip.

If we wish to guard our lips, we must control our thoughts and find the good in others. As a daily exercise in self-control, let us turn off the process of judging. Let us eliminate pettiness, prejudice, and personal offense from our minds and emotions, then higher, purer thoughts will take their place and kind words will proceed from our mouths. Likewise, if we search for and draw out the latent good instead of focusing on someone's faults, then we will have something good to say.

Speaking well of people is also a *tasty morsel.* Kindness in speech is not just a practice; it's an atmosphere. Speaking well of others feels good and creates pleasantness between people. Talking positively about people strengthens friendships and improves the bonds between acquaintances. This practice will earn admiration and respect. Everyone will know that when we talk about someone, it will always be good.

Walking the path of wisdom . . .

1. Do you consider yourself a gossip? If not, do you participate in gossip?
2. Have you ever become aware of gossip about you and been hurt by it? Describe.
3. Do you make a concerted effort to speak graciously of others? If not, are you willing?

97.

Make All of Life a Celebration

Wisdom is a tree of life to those who lay hold of her; those who embrace her will be blessed. Long life is in her right hand, and in her left hand are riches and honor (Proverbs 3:18, 16).

The book of *Proverbs* portrays wisdom as a woman, but what of this woman? Is she a severe matron? Does she give us irksome restraints but nothing to enjoy? The broader culture would have us think that any philosophy or religion that suggests boundaries takes the fun out of life. But is this true of wisdom?

Wisdom's limits are not meant to make living dismal, but to keep us from life's harm and direct us to life's good. Far from the image of a sullen hag, wisdom is portrayed as a heavenly queen who delights in dispensing her treasures. From one hand, she extends to us *long life*; from the other hand, she offers *riches and honor*.*

Wisdom presents us with a long life, which does not refer to the length but to fullness. Unlike other sustaining influences, wisdom does not offer some meaningless, impersonal force. Rather, she is a sustaining, personal power, one that enlivens during refreshment, strengthens in responsibility, and supports amid trials. More than anything or anyone else, wisdom makes life worthwhile.

When we hear that wisdom extends riches and honor, we tend to think of bank accounts full of money and cellars full of wine. True, wisdom's way may lead to material prosperity, but it's not guaranteed. The point is more that wisdom is compatible with material things. Wisdom is not an ascetic who places spiritual values in opposition to the material. In fact, enjoying the material is a concrete instance of enjoying wisdom (as long as the enjoyment is within wisdom's limits).

There is one condition to receive her treasures: We need to *embrace her*. In other words, we need to accept her ways, including her limits. Only the soul who takes hold of the beloved woman wisdom, in spite of the world's attempt to loosen the embrace, will receive her rewards. Furthermore, it will probably take an ongoing effort to hold fast and live according to her sound judgment.

Grab hold of wisdom, and you will take hold of an enriched life. Life is to be celebrated, and those who embrace wisdom and her way of living celebrate by eating from the *tree of life*. When you eat the fruit from wisdom's tree, you will taste of life to the fullest.

See also entry 41.

Walking the path of wisdom . . .

1. Is your life fulfilling? If not, what is missing?
2. What have you found to be most fulfilling in your life? Can you recall an experience that represents real living for you? How about real dying?
3. Do you recognize that placing limits on pleasure can actually lead to greater fulfillment?

NOTES:

* Whoever this person is, she calls out to humanity, offering gifts more valuable than silver and gold. Since she offers these amazing gifts, wouldn't it be great to know who she is. You can *Meet the Incarnation of Wisdom* in this free article at my resource page: www.ThePathofWisdom.com/resources.htm.

98.

Don't Lean on Your Own Understanding

Lean not on your own understanding. In all your ways acknowledge him, and he will make your paths straight (Proverbs 3:5b–6, NIV).

I know it's hard to accept, especially for me, but all the evidence suggests that we are finite beings. We lack the ability to see and know every contingency and outcome. We are incapable of seeing the entire picture. Our understanding is limited. If we trust solely in our own understanding, we will invariably make poor choices.

There is only one infinite person, knowing and seeing all. The Hebrew wisdom teachers called upon their kinsmen to lean on the personal, living, and infinite God for understanding. God is the *him* we should lean on.

How does one lean upon God? The answer according to the Hebrew sages is something called the *fear of God*. What does it mean to fear God? The fear of God does not mean we cower from him, but that we give God the place of preeminence in our daily lives.

An example from my life may help to explain. One summer I spent an entire day tiling a floor. I desperately wanted to finish so I could make it to a much-anticipated spiritual retreat that same night. But nothing was going my way. The more things went wrong, the more frustrated I became. I yelled, cursed, and tossed tools. The more agitated I became, the more things went flying. Missing out on a retreat might seem like a small thing, but it's the small things upon which we hang. In my limited view, I was unable to control what was going wrong or see that the situation was really a small matter.

If I had to do my terrible tiling day again, I would handle the situation differently—calmly, peacefully, even majestically (be above it all). How? I would let God take control of the situation.

Let him lay the tile, so to speak. This is the fear of God, such an awareness of the greatness of God that we give him the proper place in every situation and decision. *In all your ways acknowledge him.* God is more than big enough to handle any situation.

When we spend each day without awareness of the greatness of God, we live according to our own limited understanding. When it comes to situations and decisions, big or small, let's give thought to God. Lean upon him for understanding, and *he will make your paths straight.*

Walking the path of wisdom . . .

1. Do you recognize the limits of your own understanding? What are some areas in which you could lean more on God?
2. Have you experienced moments when everything appears to be going wrongly, only to discover that the circumstances could not have unfolded better?
3. Do you believe there is an all-knowing God who cares for you and has a plan for your life? How does this awareness affect your life?

99.

Preserve What You've Learned From Your Parents

My son [daughter], keep my words and treasure my instruction. Heed my commands, and you will live; preserve my teachings as the apple of your eye (Proverbs 7:1–2).

In this proverb, Solomon urges his son to treasure his instruction. *The apple of your eye* is an expression for the eye's center, the pupil. Great care is needed to protect this tender part. With this same care, preserve the instruction you have received from your parents.

Both my mom and dad have been immensely valuable in my personal development, but during the writing of this book, my dad passed away.* When trained physicians, skilled surgeons, devoted nurses, and others, who had tried to prolong his life, said nothing more could be done, then our family surrendered to the inevitable, and my dad, Charlie, surrendered to the voice of God calling him home to a place of rest and peace.

My dad, a hardworking man, something he picked up from his dad, had an unusual ability when it came to working with his hands. While I never picked up his inclination for the mechanical, I still learned much from him.

Since my dad was in the army, he tried to teach us kids to make our beds so tightly that we could bounce a quarter off of them. Needless to say, we weren't quite up to military standards, but my dad certainly was. Everyone who knew my dad, worked with him, or served under him, including me, felt the impact of his strong personality—the strong, silent type. He was a man like many men—a good man but a man of contradictions.

Despite some inconsistencies, I had much to treasure from my dad. He taught me that I was fortunate to live in this great country and to never do anything halfway. He trained me to work hard but also reminded me not to take myself or life too seriously—a lesson I'm still trying to learn. He taught me to keep the Hunt family name, and by that, he meant I should keep my word and deal honestly with people.

The proverb urges us to take as much care with our parent's instruction as we would with our pupils. I remain a work in progress, but the more I treasure, preserve, and practice anything I have learned from my dad (and mom), the better my life and character becomes.

Walking the path of wisdom . . .

1. Have you paid sufficient heed to the instruction of your parents? Why or why not?
2. Do you recognize the value of the life lessons that your parents typically possess?
3. Are you willing to reflect on the words of your parents, drawing from them those lessons that can only come from time and experience?

NOTES:

* My relationship with my dad had many positives, but it was also occasionally strained. After my dad's memorial service, several people mentioned how the eulogy had helped them to find some peace regarding their strained relationship with their deceased parent. I offer the manuscript of that eulogy to anyone who shares a similar loss and a similar strained relationship. Just maybe, it will also help you to find some peace. Download *When Trained Physicians* free at: www.ThePathofWisdom.com/resources.htm.

100.

We Are a Reflection of Our Parents

The son who gathers crops in the summer acts wisely, but he who sleeps during the harvest is a son who reflects shamefully (Proverbs 10:5).

The summer and the winter come and go, and the seasons return every year. This unrelenting advance of time frightens me; there's no way to stop it. Time is like a rushing river that wipes away everything in its path. Each day is another day that has been carried away by time's currents into the sea of infinity, and it seems I have little to show for it, except for the inevitable signs of aging, like my graying hair or balding head.

How do we make the most of these days while we still have them? We make the most of them by becoming a son or daughter who *acts wisely*, by becoming a better person—one who knows the seasons and occasions of life when they arrive, as well as what actions or attitudes are fitting.

My dad tried to tell to me one day why it was that he spoke to me harshly on occasion, and it had something to do with trying to make me into be a better man. While I don't agree with the method, I can appreciate the intent. My dad wanted me to be a man that *acts wisely* instead of *reflects shamefully*. I want to be a son, who, by the proper actions in the various seasons of life, continues the memory of my father with honor and not shame.

My dad, a good man, nonetheless had his faults,* and his shortcomings are also mine to some degree. If I deny his failings, then I am destined to repeat them. Instead, I accept them, embrace them, and bring such shortcomings under the submission of a strong character, strengthened by the might of inner fortitude. By embracing and submitting his faults, his faults die in me, and I resist bringing him shame.

No man (or woman) is ever the sum of his faults, and to make a person such is to give in to the baser aspects of ourselves. We are nobler people when we recognize what is good in others. Thus, I realize and welcome my dad's many strengths. By embracing and acting according to his finer qualities, his strengths live in me, and I reflect honorably upon him.

I miss my dad, and now that he is gone, I hope to be the wise son and better man he sought to make me. Grief and loss, while less than desirable instruments, may yet create in me that improved person—a son who *acts wisely* according to the seasons, reaping and sleeping when it is fitting.

Walking the path of wisdom . . .

1. Do you honor your mother and father by your behavior? How does this manifest itself?
2. Has time changed your character for the better, or have you remained largely unchanged? Why?
3. Do you recognize weaknesses in your character that were picked up from your parents? If so, do you realize that you honor them by making improvements in these areas?

NOTES:

* Transformative change can be elusive, even for people with a serious commitment to bettering themselves. A key reason is that our unhealthy beliefs govern our actions. Changing the way we view ourselves and our reality is essential to lasting change. *Affirming the Path* will assist you in creating the right inner framework necessary for living out wisdom's principles. Visit my page at: www.ThePathofWisdom.com/resources.htm.

Conclusion

Congratulations! By reading and applying the principles and practices in these pages, you have started on the path of wisdom. While you have finished reading this book, you are only just beginning your progress in making the ways of wisdom an integral part of yourself and life.

A more fulfilled person and a more rewarding life awaits you, as long as you conscientiously continue the principles and practices of wisdom.* Return to those entries that have spoken to you the most or that you find the most challenging to accomplish. Revisit them. Reapply them. Do whatever it takes to internalize them, and the end result will be a new character and life.

Whether we're talking about the issues of success, work, wealth, self, family, or friends, among other areas, hopefully now, you're blazing a trail of satisfaction and contentment rarely discovered in this world. This is the most exciting adventure of all your days, an adventure that entails moving toward and ultimately arriving at your better self, and all that this new you can provide in personal satisfaction and relational enrichment.

Fortunately, our journey together need not cease with this book. You have been gracious enough to allow me to travel with you this far toward a better way, and I wish to be with you further down this path.

If you purchased this book directly from me or Upper Gate Publishing, you will hear from me every now and then about how you might further your quest for peace and satisfaction in all things. If, however, you didn't get this book from me, maybe you picked it up in a bookstore or library or received it as a gift, then you can reach me by e-mail (john@pathofwisdom.com).

Nothing would please me more than to learn how you have benefited from this book and to learn new ideas and practices of wisdom from you, my new friend. (I also frequent Black Bear Coffee Lodge in Colorado Springs, Colorado. Anytime you're in the neighborhood, please feel free to stop by and if I'm there, say hi, and ask me questions or share your journey. I'd be honored to hear from you.)

Till then: *May the Lord, who is behind these sayings as well as your life, bless you and keep you. May he make his face shine upon you and give you lasting peace and satisfaction.*

NOTES:

* Sustaining real or transformative change is difficult, even for people with a serious commitment to personal change. A key reason is that unhealthy thoughts and beliefs govern our actions and work against any lasting personal improvement. *Affirming the Path*, the companion to *The Path of Wisdom*, will assist you in creating the proper inner "framing" for consistently living out the principles and practices of *The Path of Wisdom*. Find it at the back of the book or at: www.ThePathofWisdom.com/resources.htm.

Postlude

Meet the Incarnation of Wisdom

On the heights along the way, where the paths meet, Wisdom takes her stand. She calls out and raises her voice to all humanity, "Choose my instruction over silver; my knowledge instead of gold" (Proverbs 8:2, 4, 11).

Instruction, guidance, or wisdom is usually understood as a set of rational concepts or principles. Wisdom, however, is not solely rationalistic. The ancient sages of the Hebrew tradition regularly personified the idea of wisdom, as with the verses above. Since personified wisdom calls out to all humanity, offering gifts more valuable than silver or gold to all who choose her, it would be useful to know who she is and how we might come to meet her.

This woman is initially introduced to us as a town crier (Proverbs 1:20–33). She calls aloud in the streets; she raises her voice in the public squares; she warns all who are wise enough to listen: "Do not reject my words." And in Proverbs 8, the woman continues to call out. She implores in the streets and the marketplace; she pleads on the heights along our way.

Who is this person who raises her voice to all humanity? One proverb (2:6) says that the Lord gives wisdom, but in our verses, wisdom offers herself. These two ideas are complementary, and suggest that there is a close connection between God and wisdom. But what is the nature of this association?

You can find the answer in the entire postlude available among other free materials at *The Path of Wisdom* resource page: www.ThePathofWisdom.com/resources.htm.

About the Author

Why is my life a mess? Why hasn't my life gone like I expected? Many times I have asked myself these questions (or something similar), and over the past ten years, I have sought answers.

The reason that chaos or misery riddled much of my past is not because of hardships or failures. After all, everyone has those, including people whose lives are not characterized by disorder. Rather, my problem was my reactions. Typically, I responded to difficult situations in unhealthy ways or with destructive choices.

Frankly, I got sick of the same old outcomes and decided there had to be a better way. My quest for a better life has led me down a number of trails, but none more beneficial than *The Path of Wisdom*. Now each day I awake with a different question in the forefront of my mind: How can I become a better person, and how can I assist others in becoming better themselves?

Hopefully, I have begun to answer the first question, and while I have not arrived, my progress in following wisdom's way has created a much-improved person and more fulfilling life.

Through teaching, speaking, counseling, and writing, I'm answering the second question. This book is one more step in that process of assisting and empowering others to live the productive and rewarding life they have always wanted but believed was outside their grasp.

For much of my life, I have been a teacher, from the church sanctuary to middle school and college classrooms, but actually, I consider myself a student of life, wisdom, and her ways. After all, only the student grows in wisdom and is able to teach others.

I know all too well the characteristic frustrations and irritations that come with any attempt to live well. For that reason, when you make headway, I would love to know of your progress. Contact me via e-mail (john@thepathofwisdom.com) to let me know about your journey. Occasionally, you can also find me at

Black Bear Coffee Lodge in Colorado Springs, Colorado. If I'm there, feel free to share with me your journey or ask me questions.

Your fellow traveler down the path of wisdom,
John

P.S. If you would like to have me speak at a seminar, conference, retreat, organization, or church, reach me by e-mail at: john@pathofwisdom.com.

Works Used

Arnot, William. *Studies in Proverbs: Laws from Heaven for Life on Earth*. Grand Rapids, MI: Kregel Publications, 1978.

Atkinson, David John. *The Message of Proverbs: Wisdom for Life*. Leicester, England: Inter-Varsity, 1996.

Bridges, Charles. *A Modern Study in the Book of Proverbs: Charles Bridges' Classic*. Ed. George F. Santa. Fenton, MI: Mott Media, 1978.

Collins, John Joseph. *Proverbs, Ecclesiastes*. Atlanta, GA: John Knox, 1980.

Gordon, S. D. *Quiet Talks on Personal Problems*. New York: A.C. Armstrong & Son, 1907.

Hicks, Robert. *In Search of Wisdom: Timeless Insights for the Practice of Life*. Colorado Springs, CO: NavPress, 1995.

Jordan, William George. *The Kingship of Self-control: Individual Problems and Possibilities*. New York: F.H. Revell, 1899.

Jordan, William George. *The Power of Purpose*. New York: Fleming H. Revell, 1910.

Kroll, Woodrow Michael. *Proverbs: God's Guide for Life's Choices*. Lincoln, NE: Back to the Bible, 1996.

Miller, Kathy C. *The Useful Proverbs*. Grand Rapids, MI: World Pub., 1997.

"Proverbs Study Interface." *Cofcnet.org*. 2008. Web. 01 Feb. 2008. http://cofcnet.org/PSI2/proverbindex.html.

Voorwinde, Stephen. *Wisdom for Today's Issues: A Topical Arrangement of the Proverbs*. Phillipsburg, NJ: P & R Publishing, 1982.

Subject Index

Use the subjects below for personal or group study. For a group study that meets once a week, you could use an entry per week, or instead of studying a single entry, consider using a subject per week. Some subjects might naturally go together under a broader issue. For instance, for a series of weekly studies on the issue of materialism, you could use the subjects Wisdom and Work, Wisdom and Success, Wisdom and Wealth, Wisdom and Purpose, Wisdom and Charity, and Wisdom and Living.

Live Well Catalog

The Path of Wisdom
A Practical Guide for Extraordinary Living

Life does NOT have to be messed up—Really!

Did you find *The Path of Wisdom* helpful? Do you need your own copy? Do you want to get a copy for a friend or relative? Well, you can.

Simply use one of the order forms in back of the book or order online, and you'll help yourself, a friend, or a relative deal with the adversity or insecurity of life. More important, master wisdom's way and you or they will garner contentment and strength in any situation, and build confidence and composure with all people.

You or the fortunate person who receives *The Path of Wisdom* will live with surprising ease when it comes to:

- *Wealth:* invest your life doing what you love ○ add wealth without adding complications ○ want what you have ○ acquire true and lasting wealth
- *Friendship:* foster good relationships by seeing good in others ○ kind and genuine words bring amazing results ○ always speak well of others ○ practice true listening by doing
- *Confidence*: secure positions of strength with humility ○ resist the influence of destructive tendencies ○ believe that you belong and you will
- *Words:* use the power of the tongue to your advantage ○ speak forth the good in your heart ○ get heard by not always speaking your opinion

The Path of Wisdom offers gentle, supportive, but powerful suggestions on relationships, finances, success, purpose, pleasure, work, and stress, among others, leading to true wealth and lasting peace.

A better life for you or someone you know is available. You or they can have lasting peace and true wealth. Get as many copies as you need to empower yourself or someone else.

B1: The Path of Wisdom 14.95

Affirming the Path
Inside-Out Transformation for Lasting Change

As you probably already know, sustaining real or transformative change is difficult, even for people with a serious commitment to bettering themselves. For instance, gaining dominion over our wants or needs can be elusive. Becoming a person of character can be elusive. A satisfying and rewarding life can be elusive. Freedom from chaos and frenzy can be . . . you guessed it—elusive.

Why is real and lasting change so hard to make an integral part of our lives? A key reason is that unhealthy beliefs and thoughts govern our actions and work against any lasting personal improvement. Changing the way we view ourselves and our reality is essential to lasting change.

Affirming the Path, the companion to *The Path of Wisdom*, will assist you in creating the proper inner "framing" needed for consistently living out the principles and practices of *The Path of Wisdom*. Nearly all lasting change begins within and then manifests outwardly in positive words, attitudes, and actions. If we change our inner world (thoughts, beliefs, feelings), we can better live out the principles of *The Path*.

There are a number of methods and techniques for restructuring the way you believe and think. *Affirming the Path* will show you step by step these simple but powerful tools for inner transformation.

The inside-out transformation found in *Affirming the Path* has the potential to bring success, health, true wealth, and enduring happiness. The ideas, concepts, and tools in this book will enable you to:

- Replace debilitating beliefs and negative thoughts with empowering ones.
- Release destructive emotions and replace them with uplifting feelings.
- Let go of worry, embrace a new level of peace, and find a new level of personal freedom.
- Ignore your current circumstances and focus on the good you desire in life. (Your current conditions are only permanent if you let them be.)
- Control and direct your imagination to what is positive and empowering, enabling you to realize more of your dreams.
- Create greater confidence in yourself and in your abilities.

- Develop an ability to draw upon the ultimate source of strength and comfort.
- Reap previously unknown satisfaction and rewards in your life.

Affirming the Path will show you how the peaceful and satisfied of the world have come to be this way (whether knowingly or unknowingly). And now you can be among them—if you get this book.

B2: Affirming the Path $9.95

Feel Good for Good: End Depression and Anxiety

End the Downward Spiral • Feel Good and Enjoy Life
Stop Obsessive Thinking • Experience Renewed Vitality

Do you struggle with depression and other negative emotions? Obviously then, *the way you are currently doing life isn't working*—you need a change. Before you can experience a happy and enriching life, something must change.

The *Feel Good for Good* program for beating depression and anxiety gives you the tools to change your life. You can get out of the doldrums and do so for good. Live with confidence, hope, happiness, and levity.

Here's what these methods in *Feel Good for Good* will do for you:

1) End the Destructive Cycle
A person's life with depression follows a destructive cycle. Your symptoms feed on each other—like a downward spiral, perpetuating negative, destructive emotions. *Feel Good for Good* gives you the tools to reshape your emotions and break the cycle.

- Overcome a wide range of emotions (anxiety, guilt, loneliness, hopelessness, lethargy, etc.)
- Get control of your feelings (instead of them controlling you)
- Act against negative thoughts and emotions

2) Do the Things You Love
People with depression typically have no desire or energy to do anything, including the things they enjoy. Is there something you love to do but haven't felt like doing: tennis, reading, movies, music, hiking, camping, sports, writing? What is it?

Feel Good for Good will restore to you your will, your desire, and your interests. You'll soon be back to doing what you *love* (and the things you dislike, but know they have to be done.)

- Do the things you enjoy (including sex)
- Find the will-power to do what needs be done
- Concentrate, remember things, make decisions

3) Feel Better (relatively) Quickly
Most people begin to feel better about their lives from the very first exercise. This does not mean you will have depression completely whipped, but you will be feeling better almost right away.

The feelings of hopelessness, despair, anxiety, guilt, pessimism, procrastination, and any other "black hole" of depression can be defeated. You can begin to feel great in a relatively quick time frame.

- Overcome a lack of energy
- Gain momentum for the day
- Delight again in living

For your own sake, get *Feel Good for Good* today. You'll be happy (in more ways than one) that you did.

Why not put the *Feel Good for Good* self-help program to the test? I'm so convinced that this self-help guide will help you feel good that I will make you this guarantee: If you don't feel better in under 30 days, I will refund your money in full.

B3: Feel Good for Good $19.95

Master Your World
Overcome All Obstacles & Create Any Possibility

We all live in a world where we move and have our being. This world is not shaped by continents and oceans but by people and roles. The inner self is the core of life, and the outer edge is determined by the different lives we touch. Mastering this world begins with the influence and power we exert over our inner life and expands outwardly creating positive relationships, enduring confidence, and true wealth.

Master Your World is a collection of three powerful books by William George Jordan that are sure to create a more fulfilling and rewarding life.

These works by one of the finest self-help authors of the 20th century have been edited and updated to be more accessible to you—the 21st century reader.

The Majesty of Calmness: Acquire calmness and possess rare qualities such as absolute confidence, immediate inner power, and singleness of purpose, all focused in an instant for any situation or crisis.

> Calmness . . . is peace and restfulness at the depths of our nature. The fury of storm and wind agitate only the surface of the sea . . . Below that is the calm, unruffled deep (pg. 9).

The Kingship of Self-Control: Through the power of self-governance, you can pursue your best abilities and highest ambitions and realize unlimited possibilities.

> (A person) is never truly great merely for what he is, but ever for what he may become (pg. 7).

The Power of Purpose: Expertly travel the road of life (avoiding potholes, like a lack of perspective) to a purposeful destination, one of personal triumph and meaningful success. With this book, you will make your life truer, higher, and finer.

> Purpose makes man (woman) a crusader—for something. He (she) seems to grow greater before our eyes in his efforts to reach and grasp the cross of some ideal—though it may seem to us unattainable (pg. 8).

William George Jordan enables us to greatly influence our world—starting with the inner person. The same power that brings results on the inner person works mightily on every aspect of a person's life and spreads to all parts of a person's world. You can *Master Your World.*

B4: Master Your World $14.95

The Celtic Path of Wisdom

Did you find *The Path of Wisdom* a useful tool for personal growth and relationships? Then you're going to want to have *The Celtic Path of Wisdom*.

At some point we've all heard such sayings as, "You can't teach an old dog new tricks," and "What's good for the goose is good for the gander." These proverbs haile from the isles of the Celts and have since traveled the globe.

Celtic wisdom on charity—"Stretch out your hand to give, and you'll never reach out in need," aging—"The older the fiddle, the sweeter the tune," and work—"The lazy man and the poor man are two sides of the same coin," are as relevant today as they were thousands of years ago. Living by the words of the ancient Celts is sure to make modern life worthwhile.

In the same vein as *The Path of Wisdom*, this new work, *The Celtic Path of Wisdom,* is likewise bound to inspire, enlighten, and transform. *The Celtic Path of Wisdom* will send you down a way of mystery and meaning that will have a transformational effect on your life, person, and relationships.

How might your life and world be different? Well, you want the "good life," as do the rest of us, and it's available when we live each day from the same sense of wonder found in Celtic wisdom. Similarly, if you practice this way of greater awareness and wisdom, you'll sever the negative forces that bind you, and become a more empowered person, one of character, depth, and fortitude. Your relationships will also benefit; you'll add to them an ever growing dimension of peace and joy.

The Celtic Path of Wisdom will be released in late 2012. I'll gladly let you know when it is available. Just email me with words, *The Celtic Path of Wisdom*, in the subject. Or let me know you're interested on the order form when you return it.

The Celtic Path of Wisdom will introduce you to the ancient wisdom of "the misty green isles." This long, spiritual tradition gave meaning to the island inhabitants for many centuries, and it still holds value for the people of the 21st century. More personally, it still holds value for you and yours. Don't miss out on this potentially transformational work.

B4: The Celtic Path of Wisdom (let me know when it's released) ... $14.95

The True Vine: Book and Audio Reflections "Abide in Me! And Bear Much Fruit"

"Apart from me, you can do nothing."

We can't try to be spiritual. We can't even try to be good. All of our strengths and all of our blessings come as gifts from above … as we abide in the Vine.

Andrew Murray ponders this metaphor, the Vine and the branches, and takes the reader beyond mere surface application to realize the absolute necessity of "abiding in the Vine."

When you abide in the Vine, you can face bravely and victoriously life's greatest difficulties and experience the richness and fullness of life in the here and now.

In the inspirational words and pages of *The True Vine*, you learn how to . . .

- Experience God's presence and dwell in his love.
- Overcome life's difficulties and losses.
- Establish constant communion with Christ.
- Remove fear and doubt.
- Rest in God's peace and protection.
- Produce eternal results.

Murray expresses the natural fruitfulness of a life lived out in Christ, the Vine, so simply, clearly, and profoundly that you'll say, "Let the parable enter my heart, and everything will be fine." You'll overcome life's greatest difficulties and know the satisfaction of every longing.

Christ, the Vine, used this picture of a plant to illustrate the beautiful relationship we are meant to have in him. You'll find that every day as you abide in the Vine, the branch (you) will grow, nourish, and blossom, enriched by the indwelling presence of Christ.

In this special edition of the book, you also get John Hunt's audio reflections on Murray's work. These reflections are perfect for personal devotion and meditation, and will provide even greater opportunity to abide in the Vine.

B4: The True Vine: Book and Audio Reflections............................$14.95

UPPER GATE QUICK ORDER FORM
Satisfaction Guaranteed

Online Orders: http://www.uppergatepublishing.com
Email Orders: john@thepathofwisdom.com. Include the info below.
Postal Orders: Upper Gate Publishing, 6510A South Academy Blvd. #169, Colorado Springs, CO 80906

See our website for information on: Other Books, Special Resources, Speaking/Seminars, Conferences, and Life Coaching.

Please send the following Books, Discs or Courses. I understand that I may return any of them for a full refund—for any reason, no questions asked. Write number, title, and price.

1.
2.
3.
4.

Let me know when *The Celtic Path of Wisdom* is released. Email:

Calculate Total: Add up the prices above and put the sum in the sub-total. Then add the shipping and sales tax (if applicable) from below.
Sub-Total: ______________
Shipping: ______________
Sales Tax: ______________
Total: ________________

Shipping & Sales Tax: **For Domestic:** Books or disks: $4.00 for first item, $2.00 for each additional item. **For International:** Books or disk: $9.00 for first item $2.00 each additional item. **Sales tax:** Please add 7.75% for Colorado residents.

Shipping Address: Please provide your shipping and payment information.
Name: ____
Address: ____
City, State, Postal Code: ______________________________________
Phone # (required for international orders): _____________________
In case there's a problem with your order. Email:___________________

Payment:
Circle One: Check, Visa, MasterCard, AMEX, Discover
Card Number: ________________ Name on Card: ________________
Exp. Date: ___________________ Security Code:_________________
Billing Address (if different from above):

____

Upper Gate Publishing
6510A South Academy Blvd. #169
Colorado Springs, CO 80906

UPPER GATE QUICK ORDER FORM
Satisfaction Guaranteed

Online Orders: http://www.uppergatepublishing.com
Email Orders: john@thepathofwisdom.com. Include the info below.
Postal Orders: Upper Gate Publishing, 6510A South Academy Blvd. #169, Colorado Springs, CO 80906

See our website for information on: Other Books, Special Resources, Speaking/Seminars, Conferences, Life Coaching.

Please send the following Books, Discs or Courses. I understand that I may return any of them for a full refund—for any reason, no questions asked. Write number, title, and price.

1.
2.
3.
4.

Let me know when *The Celtic Path of Wisdom* is released. Email:

Calculate Total: Add up the prices above and put the sum in the sub-total. Then add the shipping and sales tax (if applicable) from below.
Sub-Total: ______________
Shipping: _______________
Sales Tax: ______________
Total: __________________

Shipping & Sales Tax: **For Domestic:** Books or disks: $4.00 for first item, $2.00 for each additional item. **For International:** Books or disk: $9.00 for first item $2.00 each additional item. **Sales tax:** Please add 7.75% for Colorado residents.

Shipping Address: Please provide your shipping and payment information.
Name: ____
Address: ____
City, State, Postal Code: ____
Phone # (required for international orders): ___________________________
In case there's a problem with your order. Email:______________________

Payment:
Circle One: Check, Visa, MasterCard, AMEX, Discover
Card Number: _________________ Name on Card: _________________
Exp. Date: ____________________ Security Code:__________________
Billing Address (if different from above):

____

Upper Gate Publishing
6510A South Academy Blvd. #169
Colorado Springs, CO 80906

UPPER GATE QUICK ORDER FORM
Satisfaction Guaranteed

Online Orders: http://www.uppergatepublishing.com
Email Orders: john@thepathofwisdom.com. Include the info below.
Postal Orders: Upper Gate Publishing, 6510A South Academy Blvd. #169, Colorado Springs, CO 80906

See our website for information on: Other Books, Special Resources, Speaking/Seminars, Conferences, Life Coaching.

Please send the following Books, Discs or Courses. I understand that I may return any of them for a full refund—for any reason, no questions asked. Write number, title, and price.

1.
2.
3.
4.

Let me know when *The Celtic Path of Wisdom* is released. Email:

Calculate Total: Add up the prices above and put the sum in the sub-total. Then add the shipping and sales tax (if applicable) from below.
Sub-Total: ______________
Shipping: ______________
Sales Tax: ______________
Total: ______________

Shipping & Sales Tax: **For Domestic:** Books or disks: $4.00 for first item, $2.00 for each additional item. **For International:** Books or disk: $9.00 for first item $2.00 each additional item. **Sales tax:** Please add 7.75% for Colorado residents.

Shipping Address: Please provide your shipping and payment information.
Name: ____
Address: ____
City, State, Postal Code: ______________________________
Phone # (required for international orders): ______________
In case there's a problem with your order. Email:______________

Payment:
Circle One: Check, Visa, MasterCard, AMEX, Discover
Card Number: _________________ Name on Card: ______________
Exp. Date: ____________________ Security Code:______________
Billing Address (if different from above):

____

Upper Gate Publishing
6510A South Academy Blvd. #169
Colorado Springs, CO 80906

UPPER GATE QUICK ORDER FORM
Satisfaction Guaranteed

Online Orders: http://www.uppergatepublishing.com
Email Orders: john@thepathofwisdom.com. Include the info below.
Postal Orders: Upper Gate Publishing, 6510A South Academy Blvd. #169, Colorado Springs, CO 80906

See our website for information on: Other Books, Special Resources, Speaking/Seminars, Conferences, Life Coaching**.**

Please send the following Books, Discs or Courses. I understand that I may return any of them for a full refund—for any reason, no questions asked. Write number, title, and price.

1.
2.
3.
4.

Let me know when *The Celtic Path of Wisdom* is released. Email:

Calculate Total: Add up the prices above and put the sum in the sub-total. Then add the shipping and sales tax (if applicable) from below.
Sub-Total: ______________
Shipping: ______________
Sales Tax: ______________
Total: ______________

Shipping & Sales Tax: **For Domestic:** Books or disks: $4.00 for first item, $2.00 for each additional item. **For International:** Books or disk: $9.00 for first item $2.00 each additional item. **Sales tax:** Please add 7.75% for Colorado residents.

Shipping Address: Please provide your shipping and payment information.
Name: ____
Address: ____
City, State, Postal Code: ______________________________
Phone # (required for international orders): ______________
In case there's a problem with your order. Email:______________

Payment:
Circle One: Check, Visa, MasterCard, AMEX, Discover
Card Number: ________________ Name on Card: ______________
Exp. Date: ___________________ Security Code:______________
Billing Address (if different from above):

____

Upper Gate Publishing
6510A South Academy Blvd. #169
Colorado Springs, CO 80906